SIMPLE PRINCIPLES™
TO EXCEL AT YOUR JOB

Alex A. Lluch
Author of Over 3 Million Books Sold!

WS Publishing Group
San Diego, California

SIMPLE PRINCIPLES™
TO EXCEL AT YOUR JOB

By Alex A. Lluch

Published by WS Publishing Group
San Diego, California 92119
Copyright © 2008 by WS Publishing Group

Designed by WS Publishing Group:
David Defenbaugh

For Inquiries:
Logon to www. WSPublishingGroup.com
E-mail info@WSPublishingGroup.com

ISBN 13: 978-1-934386-27-9

Printed in China

TABLE OF CONTENTS

Introduction 5

Lessons for Excelling at Your Job 13

Maximizing the Benefits of this Book 19

Developing Good Work Habits 21

Managing Your Time 41

Gaining the Respect of Others 57

Becoming a Team Player 73

Building Communication Skills 87

Avoiding Workplace Pitfalls 107

Avoiding Burnout 123

Getting Promoted 139

Negotiating a Raise or Promotion 155

Developing Leadership Skills 171

Mastering Public Speaking and Presentation Skills 189

Balancing Work and Family Life 205

Pursuing Education and Professional Advancement......... 223

Changing Careers... 239

Additional Information and Ideas 257

Conclusion..267

INTRODUCTION

In decades past, excelling at one's job was not as critical is it is today. Men and women tended to stick with the same company, or even the same position, for the duration of their entire professional lives. Thus the incentive to outperform and challenge themselves, or to gain ground breaking experience, was almost non-existent, because there was little to be gained from going the extra mile.

However, in the 21st century, excelling at one's job is no longer a rote exercise or even simply a point of pride: it is a matter of survival. More Americans are educated than ever before—this means more people are competing for the highest paying and most stimulating jobs. Furthermore, global trends such as outsourcing have made the job market more competitive for and even threatening to Americans. In 2007, for example, the Economic Policy Institute reported that China's 2001 entrance into the World Trade Organization resulted in the loss of 1.8

million American jobs. Indeed, thousands of American places of business have closed only to reopen in foreign lands such as India, Singapore, China, and Mexico where factories and offices are cheaper to run and staff. The combination of these forces has crunched the American worker, making the best jobs more scarce and harder to get. But don't worry—*Simple Principles™ to Excel at Your Job* will help you get the critical advantage that is now required to succeed professionally.

Many people believe their ability to excel at their job is limited by their natural talents, abilities, educational past, and even their genetics. Nothing could be further from the truth! Every single worker can excel at their job provided they are willing to follow the principles contained in this book. This book will teach you habits and attitudes that will improve your ability to manage your time, be a team player, communicate well, become organized, adopt responsibility, cope with work overload and burnout, set sound professional goals, and get promoted.

Adopting these habits will absolutely result in your improved performance in your professional life. You may be surprised where this newfound success might take you. Have you always thought you were not smart enough to start your own business? Not enough of a leader to be manager of your department? Think again—all it takes is applying the principles in this book. Is it your dream to become a CEO? A wealthy entrepreneur who works from home? A key player in your company or organization? You have the power to get there, and you will reach your goal by following the wisdom of these principles.

What is this book about?

In short, this is a book about becoming a better worker. In more depth, this is a book about developing a deep appreciation and respect for your career, and cultivating the habits that can achieve this mind set. It is about learning new skills, including listening, speaking publicly, giving presentations, becoming technologically savvy, and earning the respect of others.

This book also offers information on how to juggle your professional life with your family life, resulting in a healthy, productive, and balanced career. It is about avoiding common workplace pitfalls that have been the downfall of many an employee. Finally, this book is about maximizing your brainpower, self-esteem, mental faculties, and working environment to result in a more fulfilling, more productive, and more successful career. Use this book as a tool to help you become the worker you have always wanted to be.

It is important to remember that your performance at work will likely have ups and downs. It is impossible to nail every project, produce perfect work, and excel in every facet of your job. Part of being professionally successful is weathering normal and natural setbacks and having patience in your ability to learn new skills. Avoid putting too much pressure on yourself—but be sure to put enough pressure that you are motivated to do your best, try your hardest, and accomplish something new everyday.

Who should read this book?

This book is for people who want to:
• Get promoted
• Earn a raise

- Fall in love with their field again
- Shed their workaholic lifestyle
- Learn ways to become organized
- Become leaders
- Avoid getting burnt out on their job
- Learn public speaking skills
- Become exceptional communicators
- Negotiate a better package at work
- Learn how to give powerful presentations
- Be respected by their coworkers
- Articulate short- and long-term professional goals
- Recognize when it is time to change careers

Lastly, this book is for people who want to be able to flip to a page in a book that applies to their situation and find an inspirational tip that will quickly put them on the road to reaping the rewards that come from excelling at their job.

Why should you read this book?

You should read this book because excelling at your job is one of the single greatest things you can do to improve your life in the immediate present and in decades to come. Even if you consider yourself to be good at your job already, there is something in here for you—an organizational tip you haven't thought of, a fact about negotiating a raise you would benefit from. You should also read this book because it combines much wisdom into easy-to-read simple principles. In general, if you want to get the most out of your career, you should read this book.

To know whether this book is right for you, here are some questions to ask yourself:

- Do you have trouble concentrating at work?
- Do you have trouble understanding your job description?
- Do you want to make more money?
- Have you been at your company for several years but not yet been promoted?
- Is it your dream to love going to work every day?
- Could your communication skills stand to be improved?
- Is there a particular aspect of your job that you shy away from?
- Are you comfortable leading others?

- Do you often feel bored at your job?
- Do you hate going to work?
- Are you burnt out on your job?
- Do people at your place of business like and respect you?
- Are you constantly late or disorganized?
- Do you have a hard time settling into your work?
- Do you have an idea of what you'd like to do in the future?
- Do you have an idea of where you'd like your career to be in 1, 5, 10, and 20 years?
- Are you worried you will be stuck in a dead-end job for the rest of your life?

If any of these questions resonate with you, read on. These are just a few of the many topics covered in this book. The principles contained in this book are researched and supported with inspirational quotes and statistical information from credible sources. Its size makes it easy to keep with you for easy reference or for a quick pick-me-up in the middle of the day. You should read this book whenever you are ready to make important changes and improve your overall professional performance.

LESSONS FOR EXCELLING AT YOUR JOB

This book addresses ways in which you can become better at your job. Before you start, however, it is important to recognize the things about yourself that cannot be changed, and factor them into your expectations and professional plan.

For example, you cannot control the fact that negotiating does not come naturally to you. However, you can control the amount you learn about the negotiating process; the number of times you practice your pitch for a raise or promotion; your ability to be flexible in your negotiations; and your willingness to ask for what you really want. Similarly, you cannot control the fact that you didn't pursue educational opportunities earlier in life; but you can control your ability to pursue them now; participate in professional development programs; learn a new language or skill set that will help your job performance; and stay up-to-date on trends and developments in your industry.

In other words, in order to excel at your job you will have to forgive yourself for mistakes made in the past and release yourself from feeling responsible for the natural limitations you have. You also must avoid letting your past or natural limitations hold you back, because after you read this book, there will be no excuse for not excelling at your job.

This book emphasizes the role that taking initiative and paying attention to detail play in your overall professional success. Many of the principles that follow encourage you to demand high quality work of yourself, to take pride in your position no matter where you fall on the company ladder. Several principles guide you away from destructive, unhealthy, or unproductive behaviors that interfere with your ability to concentrate and work. There are also principles that help you become the kind of person that your coworkers respect and your managers depend on. Finally, there are principles that offer advice on social, organizational, and personal habits to adopt if you want to have an easier time excelling at your job.

What does it mean to have a successful career?

Enjoying a successful career means different things to different people. One person might define having a successful career as one that makes her wealthy, important, and powerful. Another person might consider a career to be a success when it affords him the time to be with his family and raise his kids. Still another person might call a career a success when it enables her to travel, work from home, invent a new product, change the way society functions, or enrich the lives of others. To some, a successful career might yield a lot of money; to others, it might yield a lot of time. Others might call a career a success when they are interested in the work they do, while others might call getting the corner office, a receptionist, and a team of people working under them the model of a successful career. All of these visions of a successful career are valid for different people with different goals—and all are attainable provided you learn to excel at your job.

Let's explore what a day in which you excel at your job is really like. It is a day in which you wake up feeling excited and ready to go to work. It is a day in which you are so organized that you never feel rushed, backed into a corner, or pressed for time. It is a day in which you look impeccably and appropriately dressed to do your job. It is a day in which you produce high quality, error-free work that you and others can be proud of. It is a day in which you inspire others to excel at their jobs, and a day in which you garner the respect of your colleagues. It is a day in which you feel confident in your ability to communicate with others, to be an important member of a team, and to take initiative to secure yourself increasingly interesting and rewarding professional opportunities. It is a day in which you work hard but get home in plenty of time to eat dinner with the family, indulge in a personal hobby, and read to your kids before they go to sleep. It might even be a day on which you get promoted, earn more vacation time, secure yourself a raise, and negotiate a nicer office. You go to sleep after this fantastic day, feeling professionally satisfied, accomplished, respected by others, and excited to see what tomorrow holds for your ever-burgeoning career.

That's not a bad day, is it?

What do you need to know in order to excel at your job?

There is a lot you need to know in order to excel at your job, and this book simplifies the enormous amount of information for you. It offers the following tools to help you excel at your job:

- Advice on how to develop good work habits
- Tips for managing your time
- Ways to think like a team player
- How to read, write, and communicate effectively
- How to prepare for public speaking engagements and presentations
- How to balance your work life with your family life
- Work habits that will get you promoted
- Tools for negotiating and networking
- How to avoid making classic workplace mistakes
- Ways to avoid burning out on your job
- How you can come to love going to work
- How you should approach the process of changing careers

Use the simple principles in this book as you would a toolbox. Refer to them often as you need them. Eventually the tips in this book will become second nature and you will find yourself advancing professionally—and even enjoying the process of excelling at your job.

Maximizing the Benefits of this Book

Always keep this book handy. Keep it in your briefcase or work bag. Put in the glove compartment of your car. Stick in the top drawer of your desk in your office. Lay it on your night stand before bed. This book is written to be read over and over again. The principles will take time to affect change, so the idea is to read it and practice often. Remember that your pursuit to excel at your job is a long-term goal that will take time and effort. However, you will have to put yourself on the road to professional success the second you begin reading this book.

Developing Good
Work Habits

No one has ever excelled at a job without developing good work habits. Developing good work habits is more than just making sure you show up on time or turn in error-free work. It is about having a deep respect for and commitment to your job, and demonstrating it in every task you accomplish.

But many of us work for people or in conditions that don't inspire us to feel respect or commitment to our job. Indeed, it is much more common for people to dislike or even hate their jobs than like or love them. According to a 2007 survey undertaken by The Conference Board, the company that puts out the Consumer Confidence Index, contemporary American workers hate their jobs more than ever. Twenty years ago, just 39 percent of Americans said they disliked their job. Today, however, more than 50 percent say they hate their jobs.

Workers under the age of 25 seem to hate their jobs most—

61 percent said they were unsatisfied with their job, working conditions, and salary. Even older workers dislike their jobs: 55 percent of workers age 45 to 54 hate their job. Interestingly, people living in New York, New Jersey, and Pennsylvania are most likely to hate their jobs (only 41 percent said they were satisfied). Workers in Montana, Idaho, Wyoming, Nevada, Utah, Colorado, Arizona, and New Mexico, on the other hand, were more inclined to like their work (56 percent). No matter where they live, however, when people dislike their job, it is difficult to muster respect and commitment for it.

The trick to respecting your job is to respect yourself. Take pride not in your company or your manager, but in the job that you personally do. Feel the confidence and satisfaction that comes from doing your best, no matter what the task.

The Greek author Lafcadio Hearn once wrote, "All good work is done the way ants do things: Little by little." Indeed, developing good work habits won't happen overnight. But if you institute just one of the following principles in your professional life, you will soon develop an impressive collection of work habits that your managers and coworkers are sure to notice.

Principle #1

Know your job description.

You will be unable to excel at your job if you don't fully understand what your job *is*. Make sure both you and your manager have an updated copy of your job description. One can be obtained from your manager or human resources. Revisit this job description every 6 months. Note how your job has changed, and mark these changes in the job description. If there are certain tasks you are technically responsible for that never get done, either remove them from your job description, or delete other responsibilities to make room for them. Understanding your job description is the first step towards becoming a person who excels at—and even advances beyond—her job.

Principle #2

Just do it.

Especially if you are new at a company, it is important to be agreeable when assigned projects and tasks. There may be certain tasks you like to do better than others, but you must be willing to embrace the full responsibilities of your job. In this spirit, say "yes" to every task you are asked to accomplish, no matter how irritating, boring, or mundane it seems. In time, you can let your boss know that while you are willing to do everything your job entails, you prefer certain types of work over others. If delivered graciously and non-argumentatively, this request is likely to be honored by your boss. But until then, if your boss asks you to do something, just do it without arguing or complaining.

Principle #3

Don't let yourself get distracted.

———————————— ✳ ————————————

Writer Robert Bloch once astutely noted, "Any occurrence requiring undivided attention will be accompanied by a compelling distraction." Indeed, it sometimes seems as if the universe delights in offering up a tempting distraction right at the moment you settle down to do serious work. You will be unable to get good work done if you are prone to distractions. To spend quality time working, turn off any music that has lyrics. Sign out of e-mail. Turn your cell phone off. Avoid surfing the web. If your workspace has a door, close it to let colleagues know you are not to be disturbed. Finally, if your office is near the break room or another distracting location, ask to be moved.

Principle #4

Dress appropriately.

You might be the smartest, most capable employee in your department. But if you fail to dress appropriately, your coworkers and managers will overlook or look down upon you. Dressing appropriately for your job means making sure your successful inside matches your outside. If you work in a casual or labor-intensive environment, it is important to wear proper footwear, protective covering, and clothes that allow you to move. On the other hand, if you work in an office, it is important to come to work dressed in a polished and respectable manner. Though dress codes vary from industry to industry, clean, pressed, and matching clothes are the very least you should manage.

Principle #5

Never turn in sloppy work.

It is probably not often that you throw on some random clothes and leave your house without looking in the mirror. Let your work have the same chance to be polished and groomed before it leaves your desk. Spelling mistakes or poor grammar should not get in the way of scoring a promotion or expertly expressing your ideas to others. There is rarely a good excuse for turning in sloppy work. So, prepare your work the same way you prepare yourself. Proofread everything you write; make sure the pages are in the right order; doublecheck that all your information is correct; and take the time to present it in professional packaging. Your attention to detail could be the difference in being seen as competent or careless.

Principle #6

Be the employee your boss sets his watch by.

Woody Allen once quipped, "Eighty percent of success is showing up." Arriving promptly demonstrates your respect for your colleagues, clients, or whomever you are meeting. It shows them you value their time as well as your own. Being punctual also allows you to strip yourself of the stress that being late causes. You will never have to rush, backpedal, sacrifice, or scrimp on quality because you are under the gun. Furthermore, when you arrive on time, your appointments are less likely to run over. Being punctual is key to excelling at your job.

Principle #7

Use electronic alerts and reminders to keep you on schedule.

Not all of us have the privilege of working with a personal assistant. But these days, "personal assistants" are available to anyone with the most basic technological devices such as a cell phone or computer. Explore the features on these devices to find alarm and alert functions. Most basic e-mail programs have a calendar you can set to send e-mail reminders about appointments and deadlines. Cell phones typically have a buzzer feature you can set to alert you of an upcoming meeting or date. Familiarize yourself with these applications and personalize the settings so you never miss another event.

Principle #8

Leave your personal life at home.

It is unprofessional to bring your personal life with you to work. Simply put, work is not the place for love, sex, marriage, drama, heartbreak, finances, hobbies, or any other personal pursuit! Find professional ways to deal with personal issues. Should your grandmother pass away, for example, take a few days off to grieve; do everything you can to avoid bursting into tears throughout the work day. If you have children, parent them on your own time; your coworkers will be irritated if you are constantly on the phone with or leaving work to pick them up from school. In the professional world, the less people know about you, the more they are apt to see you as a dedicated, competent worker.

Principle #9

Keep your workspace
clean and organized.

Keeping a tidy office is not only for your own organizational benefit. It is to maintain an image among your coworkers and managers. No matter how good your work is, people are turned off by sloppiness. A cluttered desk and unkempt office indicates to those around you that you are disorganized, frazzled, even unsanitary or unhygienic. If you have a reputation for being a slob, people will assume your work is sloppy, too, even if it comes in flawlessly. Remember, your office or workspace is part of a public community—it is not only professional, but courteous to those you work with to keep it clean and neat.

PRINCIPLE #10

Take notes during meetings and consultations.

A shocking number of workers fail to take notes during meetings and consultations. Employees who do not document the events they attend are significantly less likely to excel at their job. The writing down of information helps cement it in your mind. In fact, you are much more likely to remember something you have written down than something you have simply committed to memory. Taking notes also shows your client, coworker, or boss you are interested in what you are discussing. They will remember this effort when they consider you for high-level projects and promotions.

Principle #11

Be flexible.

Lowell Jay Arthur once said, "The least flexible component of any system is the user." As a computer programming guru and author of several books on the subject, Arthur is an expert on what makes systems succeed and fail. In the system of the workplace, an inflexible worker can gum up the works and slow production. Therefore, be someone who can roll with the punches. Get on board with a new idea or plan as soon as it is introduced. Your boss probably does not have time to explain to you why something has changed, and will find any inflexibility on your part irritating and unhelpful. Help everyone on your team by adapting to changes and being flexible.

Principle #12

Embrace work you hate.

Every job has tasks that are more and less enjoyable. It is the tasks you hate most you must embrace if you are to excel at your job. Too many employees focus only on the work they like doing because it seems easy, even fun. But in order to excel at your job, you must embrace all the work, not just the parts you like best. It is OK to turn to your favorite jobs when warming up to do work, but be prepared to tackle your least favorite responsibilities every single day. As sports coach Duke Snider has put it, "What a player does best, he should practice least. Practice is for problems." As you get better at the harder parts of your job, you probably won't hate them as much.

PRINCIPLE #13

Get into a work groove.

You can be more productive in one hour than one day by getting yourself to a place of solid, Zen-like concentration, or "a groove." A groove is a zone in which you are 100 percent focused on the task at hand. You live the research; you breathe the project. Every pore, every cell, every thought is an exchange between you and your work. It is in this mental garden you become able to engage your work on a higher level. Hindu scholar Patanjali once said, "In deep meditation the flow of concentration is continuous like the flow of oil." Get yourself into a groove in which your thoughts flow without end or interruption.

Principle #14

Never skip breakfast on a work day.

❋

Ever wonder why breakfast has been labeled the most important meal of the day? The answer is simple. When you sleep, you engage in an 8 to 10 hour fast, which causes your metabolism to slow. When your cells do not receive sufficient nutrition immediately following the fast, they fail to function as efficiently. For this reason, people who skip breakfast are more likely to be tired, clumsy, distracted, and unfocused. None of these are traits you want to exhibit at work! To perform your best, eat a healthy, nutritious breakfast. If you are pressed for time, keep breakfast materials, such as cereal, granola bars, and bananas, at your work station.

Principle #15

Have the right equipment.

———————— ✳ ————————

American storyteller Louis L'Amour once said, "Opportunity knocks all the time, but you have to be ready for it. If the chance comes, you must have the equipment to take advantage of it." The same is true for excelling at your job. If you go to work lacking the proper equipment, you will be unable to take advantage of the ideas and skills being taught. Therefore, always show up with the equipment that will make it easier for you to do your job well. At the very least, this means a notebook, pens, pencils, files you need to work with, client contact information, your PDA or cell phone, a calendar, and any specialty items that relate particularly to your job.

PRINCIPLE #16

Bring a positive attitude to work.

———————————— ✳ ————————————

Insert positive thinking into your workday in the same way you brush your teeth, eat meals, and change your clothes. Thinking positively will not only make your work day progress faster—it will be evident to everyone around you that you like your job, respect the people you work with, and take your organization's mission seriously. Mahatma Gandhi once said, "A man is but the product of his thoughts what he thinks, he becomes." Realize that you are the sum of your thoughts. If you think negative, ugly, unkind thoughts about your job, you are more than likely to be viewed by others as a negative, ugly, and unkind worker.

Principle #17

Never run out of work to do.

Nothing disappoints the boss more than seeing her reports wandering aimlessly around the office with nothing to do. In fact, good employees know that even when they finish their work, there is always more to do. If you run out of work, take it as an opportunity to get a jump on researching future projects; return phone calls and e-mails; brainstorm new projects, products, or systems; or clean out old files and papers. Finally, if you are truly out of work, ask your boss for more: she will appreciate and be impressed by your initiative. Never running out of work also makes your job more secure: after all, a full-time employee who is only half busy is not likely to be seen as necessary to the company.

Managing Your Time

The American work day is typically comprised of 8 or 9 hours. Yet rarely does an employee accomplish this many hours of work in a day. In truth, most employees waste a substantial part of their workday, which puts them at a disadvantage when their employers are looking to promote and offer raises. A 2007 survey undertaken by Salary.com found the average employee wastes about 20 percent of the workday. Young people are even more inclined to mismanage their time, wasting an average of 2.1 hours per day. In fact, 30- to 39-year-olds and 40- to 49-year-olds waste only slightly less time, reporting 1.9 and 1.4 hours wasted, respectively. This adds up to a lot of wasted time on the job, and a lot of wasted opportunity when your boss comes looking for her most competent employees.

Why do many of us find ourselves so unable to manage our time? For one, our world is increasingly complicated. We own more gadgets, tend to have more to do, are in touch with more people, and have more places to go. While the Internet and other high-tech devices have allowed us to take care of certain tasks more efficiently, they have also added more complications to what might otherwise be simple, one-step tasks. The fast-paced, instant gratification quality of the information age has also cut down on our ability to focus on one task until it is complete. Thus many of us end up feeling like we are in the middle of 80 different incomplete projects, and can't quite catch a breath to finish any one of them.

Streamlining the business of life is not a skill that comes naturally to many people. Because of this, millions are spent each year on products and programs that promise to help people manage their time. But these overly complicated solutions tend to add to the problem while exploiting those who are most in need of help. In reality, there is no magic trick to better managing your time: all it takes is the will to create good systems and the resolution to stick with them. By integrating the following foundational principles with your busy life, you will achieve the organization enjoyed by people who consistently excel at their job.

Principle #18

Get a Personal Digital Assistant (PDA).

According to an October 2006 study, Americans lag behind Europeans in their use of personal digital assistants (PDAs), such as a Blackberry or iPhone. In Western European nations such as France, Germany, Italy, Spain, and the United Kingdom, 29 percent of Internet users regularly access the Web from a PDA, compared to only 19 percent in the U.S. PDAs are an excellent business tool that can help you manage your time. Users can access the Internet, manage their calendar, check voice mail, and jot down important thoughts and notes from just about any location as if they were in their office. A PDA is truly an office in your pocket. Get one in order to manage your time more efficiently.

Principle #19

Tackle big projects in pieces.

Make a big job or project seem more manageable by breaking it down into bite-sized tasks. Make a list with your ultimate goal at the top. Then, outline each step involved in accomplishing the goal. Put a line through each entry as you complete steps. Before you know it, you will have completed the job and all that will remain on the page is your finished project. By building a clear road map to your goal, you can reduce the overwhelming feeling of "where do I begin?" that often accompanies large projects. Outlining the steps involved in a large project will also help you approach it with organization, foresight, and confidence, which means you are likely to finish it in less time.

Principle #20

Delegate tasks to others who are capable.

Manage your time by leaning on others for help. As North Dakota Senator Byron Dorgan once advised: "When in charge ponder. When in trouble delegate." Indeed, the mark of a successful person is knowing you cannot do everything by yourself. Instead, delegate responsibility to others you trust. These people might be coworkers, assistants, or even family members who might be willing to help stuff envelopes or organize files. Learning to share responsibilities is key to managing your time and preventing "system overload." It is just as important to know when to pass tasks on to others as it is to complete the whole project yourself.

Principle #21

Turn down projects you are too busy to take on.

Some people are so eager to get ahead, they take on any challenge put to them. While this go-getter mentality is to be applauded, it can land a person in trouble if he is too busy to do his best work. Therefore, say "no" when you are asked to take on work that in truth you are too busy to accept. Make it clear your workload is full and you will be unable to do the high-quality work you demand of yourself. Taking on more than you can handle is a surefire way to become scatterbrained and disorganized, and threatens to ruin your reputation for good work. Your boss will appreciate your honesty and your commitment to high-quality work.

Principle #22

Group like activities together.

— ※ —

Accomplishing tasks together is an excellent way to manage your time. Before you dig into your work day, make a list of all tasks that need to be accomplished. Once you know what needs to get done, group similar activities together. For example, if you need to meet with people on the first floor for 3 different reasons, schedule appointments with all first-floor people around the same time of day. If you have clients to meet, schedule your appointments in the same vicinity, or in a time-efficient route. Mapping sites such as Google Maps (www.google.com/maps) or Mapquest (www.mapquest.com) are excellent tools for plotting an efficient route. Taking care of work in groups will prevent second trips and wasted time.

Principle #23

Don't begin a task until you are truly ready to accomplish it.

We tend to start work in the hope of accomplishing it, but get distracted before we are finished. Maximize your time by only starting a task when you actually have time to finish it. Avoid reading mail twice—open your mail only when you have time to pay invoices or read correspondence. Leave e-mails marked as unread until you have the time to devote your full attention to them. Check voice mail only when you are prepared to return phone calls. Dealing with work only when you are prepared to finish it allows you to complete a task once and for all.

Principle #24

Have frequently used items accessible at all times.

✳

The average person wastes 6 weeks a year looking for misplaced items. To minimize the time you spend looking for things, ask yourself, "What do I use every single day?" Gather those things and put them in easy-to-reach places in appropriate holders or drawers. Having to search for a pen and paper when you are on the phone causes an unnecessary moment of chaos. Likewise, frantically searching for a file before a meeting interrupts your ability to focus on the presentation you need to make. Managing your time means having important items ready to go at a moment's notice.

Principle #25

Know the supply chain.

Every company has a supply chain or a work flow. A product might originate in Department A, and then go through Departments B, C, D, and E before it reaches you. To do your job efficiently, it helps to be intimately familiar with the people who handle your product before and after you. Therefore, it will behoove you to get to know the people who work in other departments. When problems arise, knowing these people by name and job description will help you cut through the crowd to the person who can help you. Get familiar with the supply chain at your workplace by shadowing others and asking them how your job directly affects their workload.

Principle #26

Know your productive hours.

Everyone has different hours or days that bring out their productive side. In fact, a recent survey conducted by CareerWomen.com found that Tuesdays between 10 a.m. and noon is the most productive time of week for U.S. workers. Whether it be a Tuesday morning or not, learn when your peak performance hours occur so you can make the most out of your productive zone. In general, people tend to be less productive late at night and after they have eaten large meals. Save your most intensive work for the hours when you know you are most alert and ready to work. It makes more sense to complete a project in your 3-hour productive zone than to labor on it for 8 hours during non-productive ones.

Principle #27

Hold office hours.

The American playwright George S. Kaufman once wrote, "Office hours are from 12 to 1 with an hour off for lunch." Though the beloved humorist poked fun at the idea of holding office hours, they can be an effective tool for managing your time efficiently. In the typical workday, an employee is interrupted an average of 3 times an hour with requests, questions, and comments from coworkers. Imagine if you could consolidate all these interruptions into 1 hour a day! Let it be known you hold "office hours" every day from 10 to 11 a.m., or 2 to 3 p.m. Limiting interruptions will allow you to do your work undisturbed and also to give your full attention to people, which will benefits you both.

PRINCIPLE #28

Assign items their own place and put them in it.

A cluttered office is a big time-waster. Your day will progress infinitely faster if you know where to find things than if you must rifle through piles of papers and drawers to find what you are looking for. Take the time to assign everything in your office a place. Maximize cramped spaces by using tiered shelves, filing cabinets, and other organizational containers. Avoid dumping things in corners or piles where they can be easily forgotten about. Establish a logical filing system and use it—knowing where to find an important document will prevent you from tossing papers around your home or office in a panic to find what you need.

PRINCIPLE #29

Become a list maker.

---- ✳ ----

Managing your time at work can be instantly accomplished by prioritizing daily tasks in order of importance. Before you leave work each day, make a list of things you must take care of tomorrow. This should include tasks that need to be accomplished first thing, such as picking up a project where you left off, or making sure a package from the previous day was delivered. Similarly, each morning before you leave the house to go to work, make a list of tasks you need to do throughout the day. Keep these lists together in one notebook. Should you fail to accomplish something on your daily list, circle it—then place it on the top of your list for tomorrow. Maintaining a list of what you need to accomplish ensures you won't forget about it.

Principle #30

File it; don't pile it.

Lawyer Florynce R. Kennedy used to tell her clients, "Don't agonize; organize." Indeed, taking the time to organize your desk or other work space will save you hours of frustration. Take a few minutes each day to sort mail, file documents, throw away trash, and otherwise clear your desk. Create a system for storing tools, work-related items, or other supplies so you can find what you're looking for quickly. Invest in desktop organizers, and use them to keep mounds of papers, supplies, and other work-related tools orderly and accessible. You'll appreciate the freshness of a clean work space when you next return to it, and will find it easier to jump right into work instead of getting derailed by preliminary tasks.

Principle #31

Document your life on your calendar.

The famous Broadway musical *Rent* featured the following lyrics: "Five hundred twenty-five thousand six hundred minutes: How do you measure, measure a year?" Ask yourself the same question. Where does your year go? Keep track of it by using your calendar. Writing down appointments, meetings, due dates, and other reminders will help you manage your time efficiently. The minute a new task materializes, write it down! Block out enough time to work on an assignment, and when recording appointments, remember to factor in travel time. Make time each day to review the week's upcoming events so there are no surprises.

Gaining the
Respect of Others

Think of the factors that help you excel at your job like the slices that make up a pie. One slice of the pie is turning in high-quality work. Another slice or two is taking initiative. Still other slices are respecting company policy, coming up with great ideas, and being a team player. But a substantial piece of the excel-at-your-job pie is earning and keeping the respect of those you work with.

There are many reasons to seek the respect of your colleagues, but the biggest one is to influence your standing in the company. Indeed, employees who are widely respected tend to have more clout, power, and opportunity than those who are not well regarded. Sandra E. Spataro, assistant professor of organizational behavior at the Yale School of Management, and Cameron Anderson, assistant professor of management at NYU Stern, are two professionals who have studied the importance of being well-liked and respected at work.

"Individuals with higher informal status—the level of respect and prestige they enjoy among coworkers—can be at a distinct advantage," they write. "They are given better opportunities, get more support when needed, and are awarded more credit when they succeed."

Furthermore, Spataro and Anderson have found that once a worker earns respect from his coworkers, he becomes more central to the flow of office communication. In other words, he is seen as being more central, more "core", and this influences his likelihood of being promoted. Being respected at work, therefore, is more than just a popularity contest: it is a distinct indication of your ability to excel and advance in your organization.

Indeed, failing to be respected by your colleagues can negate all the other efforts you make toward excelling at your job. This is one piece of the pie you will have to master if you are to succeed in your career. The following simple principles will help you earn the respect of your coworkers so you can position yourself for great things in your company.

PRINCIPLE #32

Stay home from work when you are sick.

Absenteeism is a common problem at work. But a 2006 survey found that employers are increasingly experiencing an opposite problem, known as "presenteeism"—that is, when employees who should stay home come to work instead. The survey found that 56 percent of employers have employees who come to work when they are sick. Sick people not only have a lower rate of productivity, but also pass their germs around to workers, clients, vendors, and customers. Getting your coworkers sick is not only rude, it is unproductive for the whole company. For all of these reasons, stay home when you are sick. If you are out of sick days, ask your manager if you can work from home. He or she will appreciate your consideration of others.

PRINCIPLE #33

Extend common courtesies
to your coworkers.

Just because you see your colleagues day in and day out is no reason to let manners fall by the wayside. However, coworkers do not always treat each other with respect and courtesy. In fact, a 2002 survey by the Public Agenda Research Group found that 8 in 10 Americans believe that lack of respect and courtesy is a serious national problem. To gain the respect of your colleagues, bring common courtesy with you to work. Say "please" and "thank you." Hold doors for men and women alike. Let someone with 1 page to copy hit the copier before you. Your choice to use common courtesy will be noticed and rewarded by your coworkers.

Principle #34

Practice good hygiene.

Benjamin Franklin once quipped, "Fish and visitors smell in three days." Unfortunately, unkempt coworkers start to reek in much less time. Most workspaces are small, so it is courteous to those around you to practice good hygiene. Shower daily and wear clean, pressed clothes to work. If you work out on your lunch hour, shower before returning to work. Finally, leave bodily maintenance such as fingernail clipping to the privacy of your own home. If you absolutely must address any "bathroom habits" like brushing your teeth at work, be sure to do them inside the bathroom or privacy of your office. Remember, you don't live with your colleagues; you work with them.

PRINCIPLE #35

Warn your colleagues of potentially embarrassing situations.

———— ❊ ————

You wouldn't want to speak to a group of people with toilet paper unknowingly hanging out of the back of your pants; neither does your manager who has to give a presentation in 10 minutes. While it can be difficult to alert a coworker to an embarrassing situation, she will be grateful to you for it. Whether a person has food in their teeth, a rip in her pants, or pen on his face, take it upon yourself to inform him or her in as discrete a manner as possible. Your colleagues will appreciate the discomfort you take on to save them from a large-scale embarrassment.

PRINCIPLE #36

Recognize that your office is not a gourmet kitchen.

Just 12 percent of office workers eat lunch at a restaurant every day of the work week, according to a 2007 study by CareerBuilder.com. That means that the majority of your coworkers either bring lunch from home or order takeout on most days of the week. More than likely, the common area or kitchenette in your office is small. It is important, therefore, to practice good kitchen etiquette when preparing food during the work day. Always clean up after yourself. Never eat someone else's food or use their condiments unless they've given you permission. Finally, avoid using the common kitchen to reheat or prepare foods that have a particularly strong odor.

PRINCIPLE #37

Be a courteous smoker.

There are just a handful of states—Alabama, Texas, and West Virginia among them—in which it continues to be legal to smoke inside a workplace. Most states, however, have not only banned smoking inside workplaces, but have even made it illegal to smoke within 10, 15, or 25 feet of a doorway. If your workplace has rules about smoking, follow them strictly. It is also considerate to wear a glove or jacket while you smoke that you can remove when you are finished. The smell of smoke is less likely to linger on you, which your smoke-free colleagues will appreciate. Finally, refrain from smoking in front of colleagues who will judge you for it. Smoking is a personal habit: work to keep it that way.

Principle #38

Volunteer for extracurriculars.

An excellent way to gain the respect of your colleagues is to volunteer for random office tasks. Be the guy who offers to update everyone's contact information to create a company directory. Be the girl who volunteers to head a social committee in charge of putting on quarterly company breakfasts. Your colleagues will be impressed by your willingness to go above and beyond for everyone's benefit. Your small gestures are likely to endear you to the people you work with. As Herman Melville once wrote, "We cannot live only for ourselves. A thousand fibers connect us with our fellow men." In this spirit, go to work with the well-being of your colleagues in the forefront of your mind.

Principle #39

Become known as a go-to person.

—————————— ⁂ ——————————

Everyone loves the person they can call in a pinch or rely on when the going gets tough. Your colleagues will respect you if they feel assured that no matter the problem or task, you will do everything in your power to get it done on time and under budget, or rustle up the person who can. It can take a few months to develop your reputation as a "go-to" person. You will need to show those you work with that you are extraordinarily competent, clever, resourceful, and passionate about the organization. You will also need to be extremely consistent in your devotion to excellence. Once you establish yourself as a premiere problem solver, however, your company won't know how to function without you.

Principle #40

Take responsibility for yourself.

When things go wrong and you are involved, it is important that you take responsibility for your actions. Avoid hemming and hawing, getting overly defensive, or making petty excuses for yourself. Above all, never put the blame on a third party. Blaming someone else is a cowardly maneuver, and will make you look tacky and petty. If someone else is responsible for the error, your boss is likely aware of it, and will speak to them in good time. You will be respected by your manager and your coworkers if you show integrity by always taking responsibility for your mistakes, and never needlessly implicating others.

PRINCIPLE #41

Don't be a downer.

Your attitude affects not only your experience at work, but the experience of those who interact with you. If you feel negatively about your company, keep it to yourself. It's one thing to have a bad attitude with yourself; it's another to take others down with you. As writer Maya Angelou has advised, "If you don't like something, change it. If you can't change it, change your attitude. Don't complain." Those who complain about their jobs are seen by their coworkers as whiny and negative, and don't garner very much respect. For the sake of your reputation at work, keep your complaints and tirades for the ears of your friends, family, or your personal journal.

PRINCIPLE #42

Decorate your office professionally.

How much respect might you have for a coworker who blankets her cubicle with pictures of unicorns, kittens, and movie posters? The way we decorate our work environment says a lot about who we are. It is important to bring personality to your office space, but make sure that personality falls within professional boundaries. As such, it is okay to hang respectable photos, inspirational or natural paintings, or professional certificates, awards, and trophies. But keep your coworkers' respect for you high by taking down anything in your office space that seems overly personal, childish, or inappropriate for the work environment.

Principle #43

Don't allow yourself to be bullied.

— ❊ —

One would think the problem of bullying would end at the school playground. Yet bullying continues to be an issue adults must contend with, especially at work. A national survey conducted by the Workplace Bullying Institute found that 37 percent of American workers, an estimated 54 million people, have been bullied at work. When the studied included people who had witnessed acts of workplace bullying, the problem affected half (49 percent) of all American workers— about 71.5 million people. Gain the respect of your colleagues by never allowing yourself to be bullied—and by helping colleagues out if you witness them being bullied.

Principle #44

Be someone your coworkers can trust.

In order to enjoy the respect of your colleagues, you must earn it by being trustworthy. Being trustworthy in a professional setting has several meanings. First, it means never stealing ideas or going behind a coworker's back. Second, it means being willing to not always receive credit for your work or ideas, but being willing to share credit with a team. Third, it means keeping coworker confidences and company secrets. Finally, it means being a vault for sensitive information, and never gossiping about your colleagues. If you institute just one of these habits a day, you will find yourself enjoying the respect of your colleagues in no time.

Becoming a Team Player

In the 21st century, the American workplace is increasingly team oriented. Companies are dropping the hierarchical model of working, in which employees work alone and then report individually to their manager. The new trend is to organize departments laterally, meaning they are made up of teams that feature a cross-section of people from different disciplines and departments.

Let's say a publishing company wanted to publish a book. Under the old hierarchical model, it might assign a writer a project. The writer's manuscript would be passed to an editor, who would review it with a publisher. Then, they'd send the manuscript to production, where a graphic artist would dress it up. Finally, it would be sent to sales and marketing, who would figure out how best to sell it. Because each step of the process is separated from the one before and after it, there is not much room to troubleshoot problems when they arise.

The lateral model of working, on the other hand, would employ a team to work on the project, and as such create a product more efficiently and with greater vision. At the outset of the project, a writer, editor, graphic artist, publisher, and someone from sales and marketing would be placed together on a team. As a team, these people would work out kinks of the new book, bringing their different areas of expertise to the same table. They would envision the project as a whole, rather than looking at their one step of the process. After they work as a team, they split up to work individually, and their work is benefited by the team's comments and ideas.

The lateral model of work will be an increasingly used feature of the American workplace, and thus you must learn to become a team player. To do this, you will have to surrender your inclination to control a project and take credit for it. As Michael Chick, CEO of a San Diego-based consulting firm, says, "The fact is that no one person could have built our railroads or programmed Microsoft Windows. Like it or not, we are all team players." The following simple principles will help you understand what it means to be a team player and help you get a jump on developing the necessary skills.

Principle #45

Let your team take your idea and run with it.

When working as a team, be prepared to share your ideas with your colleagues. But sharing your ideas doesn't just mean speaking them aloud—it means being willing to give your idea over to the group to see what can be done with it. A good idea may start with you; but it may turn into a *great* idea when modified by others. Therefore, avoid micromanaging your idea, or attempting to control it. Allow your team members to get creative with your idea, and encourage them to tweak, enhance, or embellish it. Once you present an idea to your team, allow it to truly become team property.

Principle #46

Assume you have everything to learn from your team members.

The successful engineer Charles F. Kettering once said, "Where there is an open mind, there will always be a frontier." Keeping your mind open will allow you to explore vast frontiers you never knew existed. Even if you feel that you have a thorough knowledge about a given topic, treat your team members as teachers with something to offer you. Ask questions to get a perspective you may not have considered. Be open to feedback. Ask others to help you understand situations in which you might not be comfortable. When you and your teammates are effortlessly learning from and teaching each other, you will truly be working as a team.

Principle #47

Avoid pigeonholing members of your team.

Teams are made up of people with different specialties. A publishing company, for example, might put a writer, an editor, a graphic artist, and someone from sales on a team tasked with brainstorming a new set of books. Yet just because someone on your team is proficient in one area does not mean he or she will not volunteer something useful in another. The graphic artist might have an excellent idea for what to title the books; the writer might come up with a winning visual design. More often than not, the people on your team have multiple strengths. Tap into them by avoiding the urge to limit their contribution to the area in which they are supposed to specialize.

PRINCIPLE #48

Play devil's advocate.

Devil's advocate—the practice of arguing something you don't necessarily believe for the sake of exploring a point—is an important exercise that helps clarify a mind set and rationale different from your own. Devil's advocate is a method used in the top law schools in America, because it sharpens the minds of those who must present and defend ideas. This technique should be employed by teams as they hash out ideas. Get in the habit of playing devil's advocate for the people on your team. By inhabiting another perspective, you develop a deeper understanding of where people are coming from in their arguments. Devil's advocate will also expose holes in a team member's logic, helping the group focus on those areas when troubleshooting ideas.

Principle #49

Be open-minded, but know ultimately what you think.

The best teams are devoid of "yes-men." The worst are filled with them. When ideas are presented to the group, responses such as "Sounds good to me," or "I guess that would be fine," never help the team move forward with its task. While it is important to be open to the ideas of others, it is critical to know how to form an opinion that will help steer the group. As the poet George Crane once warned, "One can have such an open mind that it is too porous to hold a conviction." Indeed, remain open to the vast array of opinions, ideas, and attitudes presented by your team, but know ultimately where you stand on controversial issues.

Principle #50

Employ your best communication skills.

Successfully participating in team projects involves employing your best communication skills. These are all the skills you have practiced that have led you to become a good employee and communicate well in general with the people you work with. When working as a team, it is more important than ever to avoid being overly critical; be honest but not brutally so; highlight a positive when you point out a negative; give others the chance to speak; actively listen; and avoid steamrolling others with your ideas. Use your communication skills to create a team environment in which new ideas are welcomed, listened to, and evaluated in a supportive but decisive context.

Principle #51

Be willing to share the credit and the blame.

If your team works collectively on a project that is met with success, avoid claiming the credit. Realize that although you may have had a leading role in the winning idea, the support and complimentary ideas of your colleagues are as much responsible. Likewise, should a team project meet with failure, avoid disassociating yourself with mistakes made by the team. Don't point out ways in which you tried to steer the team differently. Above all, never single out another colleague for being at fault. Teams are inherently made up of all their players. Working as a team means being willing to share credit for successful projects and blame for failed ones.

Principle #52

Learn how to think strategically.

When the Apollo 13 mission left for the moon in 1970, its on-ground support team never could have imagined the problems they would need to solve. But after an oxygen tank exploded on board, the on-ground team was asked to make a filter that reduced dangerous levels of carbon monoxide building up in the cabin. To do this, engineers had to fit a round tube into a square hole using nothing but the materials the astronauts had on board. Thinking as a team, they came up with a filter design that kept the astronauts alive until they reached Earth. While your team may never be tasked with an extraterrestrial project, the ability to think strategically will no doubt be required. Improve your ability to troubleshoot and problemsolve by thinking strategically.

PRINCIPLE #53

Retreat with your team.

The 1st century Roman philosopher Seneca once said, "Travel and change of place impart new vigor to the mind." Indeed, a weekend, overnight, or even just a one-day get-away can refresh and bond even the most divided team. Help your team members get away from the familiarity of the conference room by suggesting they go on a retreat. The retreat could feature problem-solving exercises, communication skill-building, and trust games. Retreats tend to improve the working relationships of team members so much, results are almost immediately quantifiable. One up-and-coming organics company saw its sales increase by 48 percent and its profitability increase by 85 percent after employees took part in a team-building retreat.

Principle #54

Be someone your teammates can depend on.

To excel in any job, an employee must be reliable, dependable, on-time, and responsible. But these qualities become even more crucial in the context of working on a team. If your team members cannot depend on you to show up for meetings prepared, they will take your ideas less seriously. Your inability to do responsible, neat work will drag down the progress of the entire group. Finally, you will be viewed as lazy and unreliable if team members find they constantly have to pick up the slack on your work. If you are placed on a team, make sure you are the kind of teammate your colleagues can truly count on.

Principle #55

Learn to take rejection.

Thinking as a team is a dialectic process. This is a philosophical process invented by the Greeks through which useful thoughts are born out of the process of rejecting poorer ones. People use dialectics when they brainstorm, troubleshoot, and think collectively. Indeed, the process of rejecting ideas will help your team arrive at its winning idea. To be a successful part of this process, you must learn to allow your ideas to be rejected. Don't be put off if yours was an idea that was rejected along the road to success. Never pout, feel forlorn or crestfallen should an idea of yours be dismissed. Understand that rejecting ideas is part of the brainstorming process that will ultimately allow your team to succeed.

PRINCIPLE #56

Avoid belaboring your ideas.

— ❋ —

We've all heard the expression, "don't beat a dead horse." In the context of being a team player, this means avoid belaboring an idea that the group has clearly rejected. If you have explained your idea to the group at least twice and it continues to be met with disapproval, skepticism, or disinterest, let it go. Fighting for a bad idea wastes the group's time and singles you out as an obstinate, stubborn individual. It also prevents the group from accomplishing its goal. If you believe in your heart that your idea is worth pursuing, jot it down. Perhaps in the near future you will find a context or audience that will be a better fit for it.

Building Communication Skills

It is almost impossible to excel at your job and be considered for advancement without mastering the skill of communication. Yet, although it is something we do every day, communicating is a surprisingly difficult enterprise for most employees. Communication problems rank among the most common in workplace skirmishes and challenges. As a result, billions are spent every year on industries geared toward helping people improve their communication skills.

Building communication skills is possibly the number one thing you can do to excel at your job. People who can voice their opinions and ideas, as well as listen to the thoughts of others, are increasingly valued in the workplace. In fact, according to a recent study conducted by the Katz Business School at the University of Pittsburgh, the ability to communicate well was ranked as the single most important skill employers look for when recruiting managers and other high-level positions.

At the heart of being a good communicator is knowing what it is you want to say. Although that sounds simple enough, many of us have trouble isolating our thoughts and opinions —but if we are unsure of what we want to say, how are we to express ourselves to others? Make sure to get in touch with your ideas, feelings, and opinions *before* you try to communicate them to someone else.

Finally, it is important to choose your communication medium wisely. With so many options for relaying messages, it is important to learn which medium is right for your particular one. Face-to-face interactions are always the best way to talk about something important. Phone calls are the next best medium for talking about complicated matters, but are often time-consuming and need to be planned for. E-mail is quick and convenient, but can make it hard to "read" a person's tone. BlackBerries and text messaging should be used minimally and only for very simplistic messages, such as to confirm a meeting time. No matter what method you use to communicate, the following principles will help you become a clearer communicator, which will translate into success at your job.

PRINCIPLE #57

Excel at your job by asking questions.

Asking questions is critical to successfully communicating with your coworkers and managers. Too often we let things we don't understand go unexplained because we are afraid to look stupid or ignorant. But a question up front often saves us from being embarrassed later when it becomes apparent we failed to properly understand what was initially said. Don't be shy about stopping someone immediately when you don't understand what she means. Say, "Could you explain that a little further?" or, "Could you phrase that in another way?" Try paraphrasing what has been said by saying, "So what you are saying is..." Questions are the best way to show that you are interested in what the other person is saying.

Principle #58

Be familiar with e-mail etiquette.

With e-mail increasingly accounting for communications between employees, it is important to become familiar with the rules and regulations of proper e-mail exchange. Don't put a message solely in a subject line—this gives people the impression you are barking orders at them. Likewise, avoid using all-caps; it gives the impression you are shouting. Avoid putting people on an e-mail when they don't really need to receive it—flooding a person's inbox is rude and unproductive. In the same spirit, avoid the reply to all function when a message is better suited for one person's ears. Finally, always spellcheck and proofread your e-mails—you will be judged on their presentation and you do not want them to appear sloppy.

Principle #59

Actively listen.

It is extremely important to hear what people say to you. Too often, however, we tune out while someone else is speaking. Our mind wanders to a task we need to accomplish later, or to what our next comment will be. Practice actively listening by being genuinely interested in what is being said to you. Give physical clues that show you are listening, such as nodding your head or maintaining eye contact. Be comfortable with silence—not every thought requires an immediate response. Sometimes the most profound thing you can communicate is silence and a knowing gaze. Finally, if you are unable to listen actively to what someone is saying to you, ask to speak to the person at a later time.

Principle #60

Aim for balanced,
two-sided conversations.

Author Lemony Snicket put it best when he said, "If writers wrote as carelessly as some people talk, then adhasdh asdglaseuyt[bn[pasdlgkhasdfasdf." With that sage advice in mind, be careful with your conversations. Take care not to let them become overly one-sided or spiral out of control. Be mindful of giving everyone an equal shot at making their voices heard. If you find yourself saying, "I know I'm going on and on about this," you probably are. It is fine to be enthusiastic about the topic at hand, but keeping your conversations equal and pointed is the best way to appear effective and successful.

Principle #61

Learn to take criticism well.

Donald Rumsfeld once said, "If you are not criticized, you may not be doing much." The former secretary of defense knew something about being criticized, as much of his time in office was controversial. However, Rumsfeld knew that he couldn't always listen to his critics, and certainly could not take their comments personally. If you have a high-profile position, being criticized might just be part and parcel of having a lot of responsibility. When criticized, don't get defensive. Listen to what the person has to say and evaluate if there is merit in it. Above all, thank them for their input—sometimes a person who criticizes is just the one who cares the most.

PRINCIPLE #62

Communicate criticism impersonally.

At some point in your career, you will need to criticize someone. When this moment arises, phrase your criticism in an impersonal way. Blaming a person for poor or incorrect work is likely to make her feel defensive and scrutinized; neither of these is likely to improve her performance. You are more likely to get the desired result when you do not make your criticism personal. For example, instead of saying, "Your report was a mess," say, "I think you should take some extra time to reread your report." Rather than accusing someone of being careless, suggest he slow down and not feel rushed. Your goal is to change behavior, not to make people feel bad or self-conscious.

Principle #63

Highlight a positive when you must point out a negative.

———————— ✳ ————————

When delivering criticism, make the conversation constructive by pointing out a positive along with the negative. When you focus only on criticism, the person you critique will likely leave the conversation feeling more demoralized than motivated to improve. Therefore, neutralize the discussion by starting off with what the person is doing right. Let that segue into what else you need the person to do correctly. For example, say to your coworker or employee, "You have been great at meeting deadlines, but now I need you to improve the quality of your work." Beginning with a compliment lessens the blow of the criticism, which will improve the overall communication.

Principle #64

"Praise in public, criticize in private."

Coach Vince Lombardi put it best when he said, "Praise in public; criticize in private." Indeed, celebrate a job well done in a meeting or other public forum where you can give an individual a public pat on the back and use her as a positive example to the team. Praising in public makes an individual feel good about himself, and demonstrates to others your standards of success. However, when it comes time to criticize, save it for a private conversation in a closed office. Criticizing people in public not only makes them unduly embarrassed of their weakness, but makes you look insensitive and crass. Choosing appropriate contexts in which to impart praise and criticism is an important part of being a good communicator.

Principle #65

Pay attention to the message your body is sending.

According to the British Broadcasting Company (BBC), body language is the single greatest indicator of what we wish to communicate. In fact, 55 percent of the meaning of a conversation is delivered through body language—38 percent is from the tone and inflection of our voice, and just 7 percent comes from what we're actually saying! So pay attention to the messages your body sends. Uncross your arms. Sit up straight. Avoid touching your face or hair. Occupy fidgety fingers with a pen. Open, confident body language yields open, focused listeners. Avoid letting your body create an unconscious barrier that contradicts your words.

Principle #66

Know when to say nothing at all.

Author Dorothy Nevil once said, "The real art of conversation is not only to say the right thing at the right place, but to leave unsaid the wrong thing at the tempting moment." Indeed, if you don't have anything useful to contribute to the conversation, or don't really know what you are talking about, it is always better to let someone else have the floor. Refrain from speaking just to be heard—people will judge you on the quality of what you have to say, not the quantity. As Abraham Lincoln once noted, "It is better to keep one's mouth shut and be thought of as a fool than to open it and resolve all doubt."

Principle #67

Learn how to communicate an apology.

— ❋ —

Learning to apologize is another critical piece of communicating well. We all make mistakes, hurt others, and speak or act inappropriately at times. When a person comes to you with a complaint or criticism, your first instinct may be to argue with his version of the story or to turn the criticism tables on him. But recognizing the validity of his or her grievance can go a long way toward rectifying the situation and building healthy communication pathways for the future. Many times a simple (but genuine) "I'm sorry" or "I didn't realize" is all it takes to restore a professional relationship.

Principle #68

Stay on topic.

Knowing what you want to say, and sticking to it, is perhaps the most critical communication skill to develop. Ask yourself, "What is the purpose of my message?" Boil what you want to say down to a single, clear statement that directly tells the recipient what you want to accomplish. In doing so you remove the potential for misinterpretation and maximize your chances for successful results. To practice staying on topic, create an outline of what you want to say. Include everything you plan to talk about. Then, check that each thought or subject directly relates to your main idea. If any entry on the outline deviates from your main message, delete it.

Principle #69

Talk on your cell phone only when your attention is undivided.

Cell phones are among civilization's greatest, but rudest, inventions. *Chicago Tribune* columnist Mary Schmich has written, "Cell phones cause not only a breakdown of courtesy, but the atrophy of basic skills." Learn to let your cell phone ring when you are occupied. Letting the call go to voice mail and returning it when you have time to talk is infinitely more professional than interrupting what you are doing or failing to give the caller your undivided attention. If you must take a call, let the caller know that you value what they have to say by asking to call her back as soon as you find a quiet place to talk.

Principle #70

Choose your communication medium wisely.

In today's world, there are a multitude of options for relaying messages. Learn which medium is right for your particular message. Although e-mail is quick and convenient, it can be hard to "read" a person's tone. For this reason, sensitive or potentially controversial messages are not always right for e-mail. Phone calls help personalize a discussion, but are more time-consuming and need to be planned for. BlackBerries and text messaging should be used minimally and only for very simplistic messages, such as to confirm a meeting time. And of course, face-to-face interactions are always the best way to talk about something important.

Principle #71

Use names and repeat them often.

———————————— ✳ ————————————

Whether speaking to your manager, receptionist, client, or coworker, the most attention-grabbing word you can use in conversation is a person's name. Instead of saying, "Good morning," try saying, "Good morning, Jordan." Studies show that using people's names when you speak makes them listen more closely and endears you to them. Even when you use a person's name in the middle of conversation—"What concerns me about this, Jordan, is that..."—a person is more likely to see himself connected to the content of the conversation. In time you will find that people will take you more seriously and place greater value on what you have to say when you use this technique.

Principle #72

Don't put words in people's mouths.

———————— ❊ ————————

Good communicators avoid finishing people's sentences for them or assuming they already know what someone has to say. They know that often it is appropriate simply to listen. A pause in conversation is not an invitation to finish a person's thoughts. Give others the thinking room to say what they want to say, how they want to say it. You might find that you never would have thought of the comment someone else ends up making. Finally, people who excel at their jobs are less likely to bulldoze another speaker during the course of a conversation—they wait their turn to talk.

Principle #73

Send thank you notes and business gifts.

Thank you notes and business gifts are forms of communication that make a lasting positive impression. When you need to thank someone for something big, never leave a voice mail or e-mail. Write a handwritten card on stationary. Thank you cards let people know you value their time and input. Always send such notes after interviews and for professional kindnesses. For larger thank you's, such as in appreciation of a job referral or freelance work assignment, send gift baskets or gift certificates to tell people you appreciate the extra effort they made on your behalf.

Principle #74

Use your communications skills to get promoted.

According to a recent study conducted by the Katz Business School, the ability to communicate well was ranked as the single most important skill employers look for when recruiting managers and other high-level positions. If you are interested in being promoted, make sure your supervisors know what a good communicator you are. Make sure all communiqués to them are error-free and clear. Engage them in professional, to-the-point conversation. Speak up at meetings they attend so they know you have good ideas and can articulate them well. Becoming known as a good communicator will result in professional and financial gain.

Avoiding Workplace Pitfalls

Chances are there is someone at your workplace that you cannot, for the life of you, imagine how he or she were hired. She spends the majority of her day gossiping, making private phone calls, and shopping online. You've seen him looking at personal web sites when he's supposed to be preparing a presentation, and it seems like every other day he is hitting you up for money to support his kid's soccer team.

If you have noticed this person's unprofessional behavior, it is likely that your employer has too. In fact, most bosses are keyed in to inappropriate workplace behavior more than the average employee would think. In some cases, they use technology, such as keystroke recorder software, to keep them abreast of the web sites and e-mails their employees visit and write on the job. In other cases, they use good old fashioned attention-to-detail to snuff out employees who are wasting time. In fact, a lot can be gleaned about employee behavior simply by walking quietly around the office for an hour or two—and the best managers know and do this, or have people out there who do it for them.

Therefore, if you are seeking to excel at your job, it is important to avoid commonly made workplace mistakes. Figuring out what these are and how to dodge them is not difficult. In fact, all it takes is a commitment to avoid the temptation to be lazy, greedy, selfish, or dishonest. In general, if your behavior is something you'd be embarrassed of if your employer caught you doing it, it is wrong. If your behavior is something your employer would not mind, or would allow here and there, feel comfortable doing it. If your behavior is something your employer would endorse, you can feel wholeheartedly good about it. Use this bit of wisdom and the following simple principles to avoid common workplace pitfalls that have derailed your colleagues.

Principle #75

Avoid calling in sick on Monday or Friday.

Everyone needs a sick day now and then. But if you typically call in sick on a Monday or a Friday, your boss may suspect these sick days are being used to pad 3-day weekends and short getaways. Managers have good reason to suspect their employees are faking sick: a 2006 survey by CareerBuilder. com found that 32 percent of employees fake illness at least once a year. Moreover, 10 percent of employees admitted to faking sick 3 or more times per year. If you want to take a 3-day weekend, just use a vacation day. Avoid forcing your manager to question your credibility by never calling in sick on a Monday or Friday if it can be helped.

Principle #76

Don't treat the common area like your personal garage sale.

An increasingly common feature in workplace common areas, lunch rooms, and conference spots is a Girl Scout cookie catalogue, walkathon pledge sheet, or fundraiser magazine. Indeed, when looking to raise funds for themselves or their kids' extracurricular pursuits, many employees hit up their coworkers. While most employers do not forbid soliciting your coworkers, many look upon the act as tasteless and inappropriate. Therefore, avoid being seen as the guy who is constantly trying to sell his coworkers something. If you want your coworkers to support you or your family's hobbies, speak privately to people you are sure will be interested.

Principle #77

Look for a new job on your own time.

In August 2007, CNN reported that 38 percent of all workers have looked for a new job while at their current one. Both men and women use work time to craft their résumés, scan online job ads, and e-mail prospective new employers about interviews. Job seeking on the job is not only dishonest; it could land you in a heap of trouble should your current employer figure out what you are up to. To get any new job you will need the recommendation of your current boss, which is likely to be reduced in quality should he or she discover you are using company time to find a new company. So be professional and never look for a new job while punching the clock for your current one.

Principle #78

Save video clips for another time.

In the last few years, interactive media and video sites have changed the way Americans watch movies and television. Via sites such as YouTube, ComedyCentral.com, and iTunes, video clips, television shows, and even whole movies can be downloaded or watched directly on the Internet. Surprisingly, a substantial amount of American workers find it acceptable to watch TV at work: a 2007 MSN-Zogby poll found that 21 percent of office workers—1 in 5—have watched television at work. It is likely that your boss finds it less acceptable, however, so save the video clips for viewing in the privacy of your home.

PRINCIPLE #79

Never look at inappropriate materials when at work.

It would seem that advice such as "don't look at pornography while at work" would be common sense for those who want to excel at their job. Yet an astonishing number of American workers routinely view pornography at work. A 2007 MSN-Zogby poll survey found that 6 percent of office workers admitted to viewing pornography while at work. Most of these are men—in fact, 10 percent of men have admitted to looking at pornography at work, versus just 1 percent of women. Regardless of your gender, looking at pornography is a great way to get fired, so don't do it.

Principle #80

Never forward forwards to coworkers.

———————— ✳ ————————

We've all gotten an e-mail forward from a coworker, family member, or friend: an inspirational message involving kittens; facts about why New Jersey is the greatest state; pleas to sign a petition freeing an unjustly incarcerated volunteer in Malaysia. Some e-mail forwards have made the rounds so many times, you might have received them more than once! But e-mail forwards are not as harmless as they appear: at best, they clog up peoples' already-full inboxes, and at worse they can contain embedded viruses or spread sensitive information. Above all, e-mail forwards are not professional material—so don't send them to people you work with.

Principle #81

Avoid participating in office gossip.

If you have gossiped about your coworkers, you're not alone. More than half of all workers—61 percent—admit they have spent work time spreading or listening to office gossip. Females are more likely to gossip than men, but with 68 percent of women gossiping and 55 percent of men gossiping, the majority of both sexes do their fair share of catty chitchatting. Trading covert information about the people you work with may feel intimate and fun, but it is bound to come back and bite you. If you avoid participating in office gossip, you have a better chance of never being the subject of it.

Principle #82

Avoid making personal calls at work.

People who make personal calls at work waste both their boss's and their coworkers' time. Yet many employees take or make personal calls at work. Some employees are so inappropriate that they answer personal calls during meetings! According to a 2007 MSN-Zogby poll, 20 percent of all workers have answered a non-work related phone call during a meeting, and 17 percent have sent personal text messages or e-mails during a meeting. If you do need to make a personal call during the work day, take your cell phone outside the building where you won't be seen by your boss or disturb your coworkers.

Principle #83

Watch what you type.

Companies are finding more sophisticated ways to monitor their employees' online activity. Sometimes, they use a keystroke monitoring program—this software records all keystrokes made at a keyboard, making anything you type visible later. According to ProofPoint Inc., 38 percent of companies with 1,000 or more workers use keystroke recording software or other methods to read e-mail messages sent by their employees. Indeed, if you type it on a work machine, your company has the right to read it, even if you are sending something from a personal Web-based account. Be aware that companies in confidential industries, such as financial services and healthcare, are even more likely to monitor employee activity online.

Principle #84

Don't online shop.

A study published in the journal *Interactive Marketing* found that 72 percent of American workers have shopped online at work. Shopping online may seem harmless—until your boss catches you doing it in the flesh or uses a keystroke recorder program to review all the sites you've visited from your computer. If for some reason you have to order something from your work computer, do it rarely and quickly. A poll by the American Management Association and the ePolicy Institute found that 26 percent of companies have terminated employees because of Internet misuse, and you don't want to end up one of them.

Principle #85

Look beyond the office for a date.

———————— ✳ ————————

A 2005 survey by the career site Vault.com found that 58 percent of American workers have been involved in a workplace relationship. More often than not, these relationships turn tawdry or sour, leaving you with a bad reputation or a coworker to permanently avoid. If you must date someone at work, be sure your romance is governed by a few basic rules. Avoid being seen together in romantic moments, and never use company e-mail or phones to send intimate messages. Don't tell others about the relationship, and ask the person you are seeing to do the same. Above all, keep your romance visually, physically, and emotionally private. Only reveal it to your coworkers when the relationship becomes serious.

Principle #86

Don't confuse your work office with your home office.

In 2007 CNN reported that nearly half of all office workers—46 percent—have paid their personal bills during the workday. This is not an appropriate use of your professional time if you are seeking to excel at your job. Furthermore, paying bills at work can threaten your own privacy. Consider that increasing numbers of companies use Internet monitoring programs, which gives them access to all the sites you visit. Therefore, when you pay your credit card or medical bill online, you allow your employer to view private information about yourself. Paying bills is not a very time-consuming task—do it from your home office to reduce your personal exposure.

PRINCIPLE #87

Avoid stealing from work.

Pilfering office supplies is an increasingly common practice. Indeed, according to a 2005 survey by Vault Inc., about 67 percent of employees have taken office supplies for their own personal use. The most commonly stolen items are pens, pencils, Post-it notes, envelopes, notepads, paper clips, and highlighters. These items are taken by 60 percent of the workforce. A bold 3 percent of employees say that have stolen more extravagant items, such as chairs, keyboards, modems, software, and computer monitors. Those office supplies cost your employer money, and don't save you very much of it. You can set yourself apart from the rest of the crowd by leaving the office supplies in the office.

Avoiding Burnout

We tend to think of on-the-job burnout as a contemporary problem that results from the rote, repetitive nature of many modern jobs. Yet burnout has been around for a surprisingly long time. In fact, one of the West's classic authors, Cervantes, knew about burnout. In writing his masterpiece, *Don Quixote*, Cervantes described a man with the following problem: "He so busied himself in his books that he spent his nights reading from twilight till daybreak and the days were from dawn till dark; and so from little sleep and much reading his brain dried up and he lost his wits."

It is likely that if you have been at your job for more than 2 years, you have had a run-in with burnout. To feel spent at a job or company is natural and common. Michael Leiter, co-author of *The Truth About Burnout*, has identified 5 factors that lead to burnout. These are: failing to be rewarded for accomplishments; having a poor social community at work;

feeling a lack of control over your job; having little or no opportunity to be promoted or transferred; and having to work with people who are corrupt or have poor values.

You can tell the difference between chronic burnout and a bad day or week by paying attention to whether you exhibit any of the signs of burnout. These include feelings of frustration, failure, exhaustion, hopelessness, disinterest, irritability, cynicism, despair, isolation, and a sense of being trapped in your life. The American philosopher Sam Keen once described burnout in the following way: "Burnout is nature's way of telling you you've been going through the motions, your soul has departed; you're a zombie, a member of the walking dead, a sleepwalker."

Workers who want to excel at their jobs must be able to combat burnout, because it can needlessly drag down an otherwise promising career. To this end, the following simple principles will help you avoid getting burnt out on your job so you are able to enjoy and excel at it.

Principle #88

Stay healthy.

According to a groundbreaking study published by Israeli researchers in the medical journal *Psychosomatic Medicine*, highly burned out workers were 84 percent more likely to report being diagnosed with type-2 diabetes than those with low burnout levels. While researchers are still studying the connection, the link between burnout and diabetes could be simple. People who are frustrated, unmotivated, and depressed tend to engage in unhealthy habits, such as overeating, smoking, and sedentary behavior, all of which contribute to the development of type-2 diabetes. Taking care of your health has been proven to increase a person's disposition and attitude, which is sure to ward off burnout.

Principle #89

Ask for more work.

Though work-related burnout and stress have similar signs, they are caused by inherently different problems. Stress is typically caused by too much work; burnout, on the other hand, can be caused by not enough. Indeed, burnout is sometimes a result of boredom. A worker is burnt out on their job when they stop caring, don't feel challenged, or cease taking interest or pride in their work. Although it may seem counterintuitive, one way to combat disinterest in your work is to ask for more of it. The stimulation that comes from having a new, high-paced, important project can light a fire under a person, burning away their burnout.

Principle #90

Don't become a workaholic.

— ✳ —

Writer Margaret Fuller once noted, "Men for the sake of getting a living forget to live." Indeed, overworking is one of the fastest paths to burnout, because it leaves little room for the best parts of life. People who overwork themselves report higher rates of stress, anxiety, depression, and tend to eat more and sleep less than people who work normal hours. Refrain from working more than 9 hours a day, and take at least 1 day a week to do no work at all. Instead of working yourself to the bone, make sure the hours you spend at work are of quality. The world is not likely to fall apart if you do not check your e-mail or return a phone call immediately, so there is no sense in ruining yourself for your job.

Principle #91

Take a personal day.

In 2007, CNN reported that with an average of about 2 weeks a year, American workers have the least vacation time of any modern, developed society, compared with 3, 4, even 8 weeks in other countries with comparable economies. But worse, increasing numbers of American workers are not even taking the vacation offered to them: According to a 2006 study by Expedia.com, American workers collectively give back 175 million paid vacation days to their employers every year. If you are experiencing burnout at your job, take a personal day. Even just one day's break can refresh you and make you feel ready and excited to work again—something both you and your boss will be thankful for.

Principle #92

Work for a company that supports work-life balance.

———————— ✳ ————————

A November 2007 study by WorkLifeBalance.com, an Atlanta-based company that specializes in work-life balance education, found that 81 percent of employees factor in a company's work-life balance policies when deciding whether to take or quit a job. And the majority of Americans—57 percent—said they felt their current employer is supportive of employees' personal commitments and life outside of work. Achieving balance between work and the rest of your life is an important preventative against workplace burnout. If your company offers work-life balance programs, participate in them, or pioneer an effort to get them instituted.

Principle #93

Make friends with your coworkers.

A 2006 survey conducted by CareerBuilder.com found that 77 percent of workers experience burnout at their job. The number one reason for this burnout? Dealing with difficult coworkers. Indeed, having to get through 8 hours of work can be difficult enough—but having to do it with irritating, unethical, or even mean coworkers can be a recipe for burnout. If unpleasant coworkers contribute to your sense of burnout, make an effort to improve your relationship with the people you work with. Invite a coworker to attend a work-related lecture; volunteer to organize a happy hour for your colleagues. If you have exhausted friendships within your work group, try meeting people on a new floor or department.

Principle #94

Adapt routines, not ruts.

Gerald Burrill once said, "The difference between a rut and a grave is the depth." Burrill was commenting on what anyone who has ever been stuck in a rut knows: they are a seemingly inescapable, mind-numbing groove that can kill one's senses and enthusiasm. Feeling stuck in a rut contributes to the burnout many of us feel on the job. Therefore, organize your day so it has routine, but not rut. For example, vary the order in which you complete daily tasks. Take a different route to the cafeteria. Vacate your desk for an hour or 2 and find a quiet cubicle or conference room in which to work. A simple switch of events or change of scenery is often enough to dig you out of your rut without drastically changing your life.

Principle #95

Work in an ergonomic space.

———————— ✳ ————————

There is perhaps nothing that makes workers burn out on their job as quickly as experiencing physical pain from it. Occupational pain is a common experience in many fields. Laborers endure the excruciating pain of back, shoulder, and leg problems; office workers groan from the chronic pain of carpel tunnel, tennis elbow, pinched nerves, and other computer-related injuries. Whatever your work station, make sure it is ergonomic, or supportive of the work you do. Wear supportive gear, such as weight belts, wrist straps, and proper footwear. Invest in an ergonomic chair, keyboard, wrist rest, and computer screen. You will be able to tolerate your job better once you are pain-free.

Principle #96

Reward yourself with breaks.

— ✳ —

Many workers find a carrot-and-stick system of rewards very motivating for avoiding burnout. For every task you check off your daily to-do list, reward yourself with small, satisfying breaks. Take a short walk; chat with a coworker by the water cooler; eat a healthy snack; or listen to the radio. Don't let these breaks turn into full-fledged distractions, however. Also, only reward yourself when you have gotten to the end of a task to maintain continuity in your thought process. Rewards help break up work time and give you bright spots to look forward to—and they feel great when you know you have truly earned them.

Principle #97

Request to be transferred to a new department.

Burnout is usually a product of boredom, which can come about when a worker has reached a ceiling in his current position. If you have reached this ceiling but don't want to change companies altogether, ask for a transfer. If you have been working with clients for the last 5 years, perhaps it is time to take a more private position in the company. If you feel stuck in the office all day, ask to be given a position in the field. If you have done well in your current position, your boss will be open to finding new ways to challenge and interest you, even if that means sending you to work under another manager's wing.

Principle #98

Have friends outside of work.

―――――――――― ✳ ――――――――――

Some employees have no problem getting along with their coworkers; in fact, they may be the *only* people they spend time with. Having pals at work can help make the day move along faster—but when your social life is integrally tied to your job, it can also leave you feeling as if your whole world revolves around work. Therefore, it is important to have friends outside of work. Limit your social interactions with colleagues to 2 events per week, saving the rest of your social time for family and outside friends. Finally, avoid being social at your job every day. While it's nice to have a group of friends at work, tying yourself too tightly to 1 group of people can actually limit your opportunity for promotion.

PRINCIPLE #99

Change your scenery.

Historian Flora Whittemore once said, "The doors we open and close each day decide the lives we live." Whittemore put elegantly what most of us have come to realize: that a change of scenery can make even the most routine experience seem new and fresh. Apply Whittemore's advice to your job should you experience burnout. If your job is mobile, get out of your home office and work in coffee shops, the library, or at the park. Ask your boss if you can work from home 1 day a week, or if you can change offices. Ask to be transferred to a position in the field, or request to be assigned to a work-related trip or conference.

Principle #100

Never eat lunch at your desk.

Despite feeling chained to their desks, an overwhelming number of American workers choose to eat lunch there. In fact, a 2006 study by the American Dietetic Association found that 75 percent of office workers eat lunch at their desks at least 2 or 3 times a week. Most said going out for lunch would take too long or was too expensive. But when we eat at our desk, we tend to eat lower quality foods in higher portions. Furthermore, we don't engage in the true mental and physical break that lunch is supposed to be. Use your lunch time to get away from your desk. Even if you don't go to a restaurant, eat in the break room, cafeteria, or at a park across the street.

Principle #101

Integrate your interests into your job.

It is important to maintain a certain level of professionalism at any job. This means keeping parts of your private life guarded—after all, some aspects of your life are simply not any of your coworkers' business. But integrating some of your interests into your professional identity can help you feel less closeted, which leads to burnout. If appropriate, decorate your workspace in a way that reflects your interests—hang photos of pets or family; interesting artwork; an inspirational quote or map. Let your colleagues know you are an avid cyclist, or used to live in France, or enjoy cooking. People experience burnout when they don't let themselves be who they really are at their job.

GETTING PROMOTED

Business tycoon P. G. Winnett once observed, "When a man has equipped himself by thought and study for a bigger job, it usually happens that promotion comes along even before it is expected." Winnett was no stranger to promotion. At 83 years old he continued to reign supreme as the chairman and co-founder of Bullock's department stores chain, a popular retailer throughout the West coast in the 1950s and 1960s. Winnett and successful people like him know that the secret to getting a promotion is to deserve one.

But in the 21st century, the job market is more competitive than in Winnett's time. More Americans than ever before are college-educated, making more people qualified for jobs that pay well and have mobility. In addition, trends such as outsourcing, coupled with high energy prices, have slashed American jobs and require that workers be more educated and skilled than ever before. In other words, to get promoted, you will need to stand out from the already competitive crowd. Tips, tricks, and ideas for standing out are contained in this chapter, and you'll need to integrate them into your life in order to become worthy of promotion.

Although the job market is increasingly competitive, there are indications that management and higher level jobs will become more abundant in years to come. Indeed, this is when the majority of the baby boomers are set to retire— some have even started leaving their jobs already. According the Bureau of Labor Statistics, 32 percent of all American workers who hold full-time jobs are 55 and older. This group cannot work forever. When baby boomers start retiring en masse, position yourself to take over their high-level, well-paying positions. This means preparing yourself today for a promotion that could be available in the next few years.

Coach Pat Riley once quipped, "Being ready isn't enough; you have to be prepared for a promotion or any other significant change." Use the following simple principles to prepare yourself for promotion so when your managers come looking for fresh talent, they'll pick you out of the crowd.

Principle #102

Ask for more responsibility.

It seems like an obvious way to get promoted, but few people ask for more responsibility at work. If your manager is not challenging you enough, demonstrate your own managerial skills by asking to tackle a project that needs to be done, or show how you can improve the effectiveness of the team. Studies confirm that taking the initiative at work pays off. A recent poll that asked the nation's leading executives what they believed was the best way for employees to earn a promotion or a raise revealed that 82 percent said asking for more work and responsibility would do the trick. Don't wait for your boss to single you out for promotion: ask for more responsibility as soon as you feel able to handle it.

Principle #103

Break the company mold.

Most employees are all too happy to go along with the status quo. In fact, a recent University of California, Los Angeles, study found that 91 percent of adult workers who were exposed to new ideas responded negatively to them. But without new ideas and the initiative to see them through, the world would never change. New products and services would not be available. Strive to be part of the 9 percent who finds the breakthroughs by questioning the status quo. Look for a new use for old products or a new system to organize old standards. Make suggestions that break the company mold. The most successful people, after all, did not get promoted by doing more of the same.

Principle #104

Attend the optional stuff.

An old saying goes, "Two-thirds of promotion is motion." Get in motion for promotion by attending all meetings, presentations, or events sponsored by your company, even if they are optional. Think of it like getting extra credit. Though the meeting may not immediately relate to your job, your attendance shows a clear interest in the company as a whole. When it comes time for your supervisors to consider filling a hole, they are much more likely to consider a candidate who showed his face and familiarized himself with all aspects of the company rather than just attending just the bare minimum of events.

Principle #105

Don't wait to be told.

Think of the delight a parent experiences when she walks in her child's room to find it is already clean. It is the same delight an employer feels when an employee has taken the initiative to troubleshoot a problem without having been assigned the task. Unfortunately, too many people adapt a "that's not my job" mentality at work. Use their apathy as your opportunity to pick up the slack. Even if it is not specifically in your job description, do the things that need doing, especially if they are chronically ignored by others. As American publisher Elbert Hubbard simply put it, "Initiative is doing the right things without being told."

Principle #106

Take your current position seriously.

Everyone wants to have a shot at the top, but it takes a special person to accomplish the bottom rung job with as much attention to detail and pride as the CEO or department manager. But workers who scoff at their current job rarely impress those who are looking to promote. Instead, managers value those who do their best to benefit the company, no matter how small or large a role they play. As David J. Schwartz, author of *The Magic of Thinking Big*, has advised those who want to be promoted: "Think, really think, your present job is important. That next promotion depends mostly on how you think toward your present job."

Principle #107

Commit to doing excellent work 100 percent of the time.

— ✳ —

American business tycoon Henry Doherty advised the future managers of America: "Plenty of men can do good work for a spurt and with immediate promotion in mind, but for promotion you want a man in whom good work has become a habit." Take Doherty's cue by making excellent work a habit in your professional life. If something hinders your success, get rid of it. Avoid toxic people. Make your environment conducive to success and efficiency. Double and triple check your work for errors. Resolve to making everything you produce at your job of the highest quality. You *will* be promoted; no manager turns her back on excellence and quality.

PRINCIPLE #108

Keep a file on all your accomplishments.

---✳---

With the hustle and bustle of the workday, it is easy to let accomplishments fall through the cracks. But in order to get promoted, you'll need to be aware of every task you accomplish for your company, and so will your boss. Spend 10 minutes each day writing down what you have recently accomplished. Make a note of anything extraordinary about the task, such as if it was done on time or under budget. Keep with this list a folder of all e-mails, letters, and certificates of times you've been recognized for succeeding at your job. When your boss considers you for promotion, it will help to have a file bursting with your achievements.

Principle #109

Be mentored by someone
at your company.

An old proverb defines a mentor as someone whose hindsight can become your foresight. Indeed, making a relationship with a mentor is an excellent way to get promoted! A recent study by a high-profile business firm found that in 80 percent of all promotions (4 out of 5), the employee promoted had a mentor who was higher in the company. In addition to helping her protégé understand the path to being promoted, the mentor was able to spread positive news to others about the employee's work habits and accomplishments. If your company sponsors a mentoring company, sign up for it. If not, seek out a mentor on your own.

PRINCIPLE #110

Let your manager know you want to be promoted.

It seems simple, but one way to get promoted is to tell your manager you want to be. You'd be surprised how many employees have no interest in promotion, or wait to be offered one. In the same way you need to go out and get a job, you need to ask to be promoted. In fact, a recent poll of American businesses found that 76 percent of promotions are given to those who pursue them. Never assume your boss knows you want to be promoted. Make your objective clear. Ask what paths a person in your company can take to become promoted. Work with your manager to put together a promotion timetable.

Principle #111

Expect to do the time.

To be promoted, you are going to have to work some overtime. Indeed, rarely is an employee promoted when she follows the bare minimum of her job description. Be prepared to put in extra hours by working either early or late. You can also take work home at night or on the weekends. Without flaunting it, be sure to let others know you are working overtime. Let your boss see you leave the office with an armful of files. Leave your office light on as people leave work for the night. If you come into work early, park in a prominent place where your car is sure to be seen by others. At the very least, check email from home a few nights a week. It's a task that takes no more than a few minutes, but can show your boss the dedication you have to your job.

PRINCIPLE #112

Work harder than you've ever worked before.

Russian ballerina Anna Pavlova once said, "Success depends in a very large measure upon individual initiative and exertion, and cannot be achieved except by a dint of hard work." The ballerina knew something about taking initiative and working hard: her adaptations to ballet shoes became the precursor of the modern *pointe* shoe. With hard work, Pavlova became one of the greatest ballerinas in the history of dance. Use her as a model for making your ability to work hard pay off in the form of a promotion. You don't have to make as lasting a mark as Pavlova, but your success will be noticed by those who count.

Principle #113

Agree to be tested.

Sri Sathya Sai Baba, a South Indian guru, religious leader, and orator known for his insightful teachings, once advised his devotees to "welcome tests because it gives you confidence and it ensures promotion." While most people shy away from being tested, it is an excellent way to strut your stuff. If you are confident in your ability to pass a test or overcome a challenge, take it, and make sure your manager is watching. There is no better way to prove you have the stuff worthy of promotion than by demonstrating it to those who matter. Be aware, however, that the opposite is true: never agree to be tested when you are likely to fail. It will make you look not only incompetent, but conceited as well.

Principle #114

Continue to sell yourself even after you've gotten the job.

Selling yourself to an employer doesn't stop at the interview process. You should continuously make your accomplishments, skills, and successes known to those around you, especially those able to promote you. Without bragging, be up-front about your abilities and accomplishments with those who ask about them. Making your successes known to your coworkers and managers will inspire them to see you as a capable, can-do person—and you will be on the top of their list when they come looking for someone capable of doing higher level work.

Principle #115

Learn a new skill set.

The best way to get promoted is to learn to do something your company needs. Let's say your department is having trouble establishing and sticking to its budget. The fastest way to get promoted to budget manager is to take a few accounting courses that position you to solve this problem. There are a multitude of professional development courses you can take that will improve your ability to function as a manager, team leader, public speaker, computer technician, sales associate— or any other position needed by your company. For more ideas on adding to your skill set, see the principles in the Pursuing Education and Professional Advancement section of this book.

Negotiating a Raise
or Promotion

To excel at your job, you will need to negotiate advancements for yourself. But many of us dread it, because we are uncomfortable with confrontation. It is unrealistic, however, to think you can go through your career without negotiating. Therefore, the sooner you learn to be a savvy negotiator, the better.

It is interesting that although negotiating usually results in a better deal for you, most Americans shy away from doing it. Indeed, the majority of Americans are uncomfortable asking for more money at their job, and some never broach the subject at all. Women are particularly at risk for missing out on the potential rewards: 20 percent of adult women (22 million people) say they never negotiate at all. As a result, they earn on average $1 million less over the life of their career than women who do negotiate.

Learning to negotiate even small amounts of money can add up over the course of your career. According to *USA Today*, 52 percent of employees who ask for higher salaries actually receive them. This can translate into thousands, even hundreds of thousands, of dollars over the course of your career. Negotiating just an additional $2,000 to your salary annually, for example, results in more than $60,000 over your whole working life. That could be the down payment on a first or second home; a child's college tuition; or lavish vacations to multiple international destinations.

Some hard and fast rules for negotiating include always being willing to walk away from a deal if you do not stand to gain from it. Also, never enter a negotiation when you are desperate: you are certain to lose out if the other party senses you are at a disadvantage. Finally, come to the negotiating table armed with information to back up your request. These and other strategies are discussed in this chapter. By following these simple principles, you are bound to enjoy the fruits of a raise and promotion in no time.

Principle #116

Make sure you receive some form of raise every year.

————————— ❊ —————————

It is important to experience growth at your job with every passing year. This growth is usually in the form of raises and bonuses to your salary. But many workers fail to secure themselves annual raises. Not negotiating an annual raise for yourself will hurt you financially over the course of your career. In fact, one study found that by not negotiating a raise, an individual stands to lose more than $500,000 by age 60! Even if your boss can only offer you a small 2 percent increase this year, take it. When you negotiate your salary next year, you will be negotiating a raise on 2 percent more than you would have had.

Principle #117

Know what is reasonable and fair.

If your company only offers raises between 1 and 3 percent, your boss will be both amused and irritated if you ask for 25 percent. By asking outside of the realm of fair and reasonable, you make yourself look silly and ignorant. The only time your raise request should be markedly outside the company average is in a special situation. For example, if you were ineligible for a raise the previous year due to a technicality, it is fair to ask for 2 years' additional compensation. Or, if you have effectively started working in a new position but haven't yet been compensated for it, it is reasonable to ask for retroactive pay. But in general, your request for a raise will have to fall in line with what is reasonable for raises in your company.

Principle #118

Research the market value of your position.

※

To ask for a raise, it helps to know the going rate. To learn what people at other companies get paid to do your job, check with salary-related Web sites, professional journals, recruiters, and the Occupational Outlook Handbook published by the Department of Labor (www.bls.gov/oco/). Jobs pay differently depending on a region's cost of living, but you can establish a general going rate to take to the table. Women must especially research the market value of their position. One survey found that women report salary expectations between 3 and 32 percent lower than men for the same jobs. As a result, they negotiate less often and ask for less when they do.

Principle #119

Use what you know to secure a raise or promotion.

Negotiating a raise or promotion is much easier than negotiating a starting salary, for one main reason: you have inside information on your company. When you were first hired, you didn't know much about your company. You had no idea how large the salary budget was; you didn't know the quality of the other people working there. Now that you have spent time on the inside, you'll have a lot of information that will help you build your case. If you are one of the better people in your department, use that to secure a raise. If you are aware that other people in your position started at a higher salary than you did, bring it up as you angle for a better deal.

Principle #120

Realize it's not always all about the money.

While salary is often the center of negotiating of a raise, there are other, equally important elements that can be brought to the negotiating table. Indeed, while a salary is often the focal point of compensation, there are many other factors that go into a compensation package. If you get stuck in the money department, try angling for one of the following to sweeten the deal: vacation, flex-time, office space, commission, managing others, commute time, in-office hours, sick time, assistants, stock options, insurance, equipment, and title. You might find that being satisfied in just one of these areas will make up for not being able to negotiate your ideal salary.

Principle #121

Aim for a win-win situation.

Any raise or promotion you negotiate with your boss should work for both of you. The trust, camaraderie, and good working relationship you cultivate when you create a win-win situation is a long-term career asset. Therefore, work hard to satisfy both parties when negotiating. Listen to your boss's needs and acknowledge the value of his perspective. Then, clearly express your own needs and make sure he understands them. Ask, "How can we make this work for both of us?" The other person will appreciate someone who respects his position and will be more likely to make compromises in your favor.

Principle #122

Be willing to put in your time.

According to the U.S. Bureau of Labor Statistics, the average American changes jobs 10 times and switches careers 3 times over the course of their lifetime. The ability to job hop has offered American workers a professional freedom never before enjoyed by their predecessors. On the other hand, it has warped an employee's expectations of when she deserves something from an employer. Indeed, it is unrealistic to expect to be offered a promotion or raise if you have been at your job for anything less than a year. In order to climb the company ladder and reap the benefits that go along with being at the top, you must be willing to put in your time.

Principle #123

Practice your pitch.

Before you meet with your boss to negotiate for a raise, have a game plan for what you will say. First, list all the reasons why you deserve a raise or promotion. Put the strongest reasons at the top, and eliminate any reasons that are not compelling —it is more important to have a few good reasons than a long list of average ones. Bring with you any props or tools that can help make your case—a file filled with complimentary letters from clients, for example. Anticipate arguments your boss might raise against increasing your salary, and find a way to counter or acknowledge them. Finally, rehearse the speech you'll give at least 5 times. Going prepared to the negotiating table can only help your case.

Principle #124

Negotiate with your mind,
not your heart.

The biggest reason people dislike negotiating is because they are afraid of being seen as a grubby, selfish person. But negotiating is not a personal endeavor—it is a business one. It is therefore important to negotiate a raise or promotion with your mind and pocketbook, not your heart. Anyone you will need to negotiate with will understand this. When negotiating, emotions do sometimes run high. In these situations, take a break, grab some water, or take a walk. Remember the game plan you made while practicing your speech for why you deserve a raise. Keeping your mind in check will prevent you from reacting emotionally and sabotaging the negotiation.

PRINCIPLE #125

Don't let your gender prevent you from asking for a raise.

Though some women are terrific negotiators, many view negotiating as highly unpleasant. When asked to liken the process of negotiating to something, men in one study described negotiating like winning a ball game, while women likened it to going to the dentist. Because they dislike it, they negotiate less. In fact, according to the authors of *Women Don't Ask*, men initiate negotiations about 4 times more often than women, and 20 percent of adult women never negotiate at all. However, women who negotiate raises for themselves earn $1 million more during their careers than women who don't. So ladies, get out there and negotiate—you are worth it!

Principle #126

Be willing to leave your job if your needs are not met.

The key to a successful negotiation is to always be able to walk away. If your boss is unable or unwilling to give you a raise or promotion, you might need to leave the company to be properly rewarded or compensated. You needn't threaten your boss with this possibility, but you can make it known you are disappointed with his or her inability to meet your needs, and feel inclined to pursue other career options. Be prepared to back this change up by sending out résumés and going on interviews. Should you land a new job, give your boss a chance to match your new offer.

Principle #127

Avoid ultimatums.

Ultimatums—threats or unrealistic promises made in the course of a discussion—are a tool for people who are weak negotiators. Ultimatums are similar to childish tantrums, thrown because you did not get what you wanted from someone. People who excel at their job know how to negotiate without resorting to ultimatums. Nine times out of ten, you do not follow through with your threat anyway, which only reduces your credibility. As the journalist Ambrose Bierce put it, ultimatums are "a last demand before resorting to concessions." In other words, even if you make an ultimatum, you will probably have to end up compromising anyway. Just skip the ultimatum and get right on to the negotiating.

PRINCIPLE #128

Help your boss create
a promotion for you.

------------------------------ ❋ ------------------------------

Many jobs have built-in ceilings. Especially at small companies, there simply aren't higher positions to be promoted to. If you work in an environment that has little room for advancement, there are still ways to be promoted if you are creative and aggressive about it. First, look for a need your company has. Perhaps it could use a communications director to simplify company communications; maybe a certain department has become so large it would function better if split in 2 and headed by a new supervisor. If you are a valuable employee, your boss will want to keep you, and may be willing to invent a position to keep you happy.

Developing Leadership Skills

Former first lady Rosalynn Carter once said, "A great leader takes people where they don't necessarily want to go, but ought to be." Developing the skills to be this type of leader is within your grasp. But first, it is important to understand the difference between a being a leader and simply a manager.

Leadership guru Warren Bennis has put the difference between a manager and a leader in the following way: "The manager asks how and when; the leader asks what and why." Indeed, the best way to understand the difference between managers and leaders is to see management as a skill that offers a group predictability, consistency, stability, and organization. A good manager keeps track of his reports' workload and workflow. She keeps them on target with deadlines and watches their progress as it relates to the rest of the group.

A leader, however, inspires people, companies, and organizations to change. She offers the people around her a vision of a better, more humane world. He influences others to work their hardest, think their most creatively, and give 110 percent not out of fear or guilt, but out of a desire to move the project forward.

John Kotter and Joseph Rost, authors of *Leadership for the 21st Century*, have made the following distinctions between leadership and management. According to Kotter and Rost, leaders offer influence, while managers offer authority. Leaders offer direction through vision, while managers offer direction through structure. Leaders get people to accomplish things through energy and inspiration, while managers get people to accomplish things through planning and routine. Managers and leaders often share a similar set of skills, but leaders have that something extra that makes their people really want to go to the mat for them.

Although it is a special quality, leadership is not an innate skill one must be born with. Rather, it is a learned skill, acquirable by anyone willing to adopt the following simple principles.

Principle #129

Build morale by emphasizing rewards and appreciation.

In 2005 *PR Newswire* reported that 43 percent of workers do not feel appreciated by their managers or employers. Yet employee-appreciation is perhaps the single biggest factor in whether a worker feels motivated to do a good job and take extra initiative with his work. Therefore, it is in your interest to show you appreciate a job well done with small awards. Take your highest performing employee of the month out to a nice lunch. Make it a habit to reward extraordinary work with small gift cards or a certificate. The best leaders know to build morale among their reports by showing their employees they appreciate them.

Principle #130

Excel at your own job in order to inspire others to excel at theirs.

A 2005 survey by CareerBuilder.com found that 42 percent of employees think they can do their manager's job better. If your reports do not have faith in your ability to do your own job well, they will not have faith in your ability to help them do theirs better, either. Be a competent leader by showing your employees that you excel in your own position. Encourage them to take pride in their work by taking pride in your own. As a leader, it is especially important to avoid making careless errors or producing sloppy work. Excel in your position so there is no doubt in anyone's mind that you are the best person to lead your team.

Principle #131

Know that you cannot do it all yourself.

Bill Owens once said, "The leader who tries to do it all is headed for burnout, and in a powerful hurry." Owens knew a lot about trying to do it all yourself. As the former governor of Colorado, Owens' job was to gather the best group of people who, as a team, could help him run the state. Like Owens, the best leaders know they can't do everything by themselves. Instead of trying to overrun the show, cultivate the best team possible. Guide them to do their jobs as best as they can. Lean on them to do work in areas in which you are weak. Together, you will be able to get the project done, with less stress and time than had you tried to accomplish it all by yourself.

Principle #132

Turn fear into challenge.

The best leaders know that it is wise to view a potentially daunting situation as one they can conquer. In fact, writer Henry S. Haskins thought of fear in the following way: "Panic at the thought of doing a thing is a challenge to do it." Take Haskins' advice and turn daunting or difficult prospects into challenges you can use to build your reputation. Those around you will be inspired at your unwillingness to be scared away from large projects or intimidating tasks. It might just encourage them to do the same. Should you start to feel nervous, take a deep breath, and channel your fear into an overriding belief in your ability to rise to the challenge before you.

Principle #133

Think of your legacy.

Benjamin Disraeli once said, "The legacy of heroes is the memory of a great name and the inheritance of a great example." As the British prime minister remembered for creating the modern Conservative party in the United Kingdom, Disraeli knew the importance of always keeping your legacy in the forefront of your mind. Indeed, great leaders think ahead to the future and concern themselves with how they will be remembered. This foresight prevents them from making short-sighted, narrow, or impulsive decisions that could maim or tar their reputation. With every action, think not only of how it will affect you today, but how it will improve or hurt the way people remember you.

Principle #134

See the big picture.

To be a leader, it is necessary to see the organization, project, or endeavor of which you are in charge as a whole. Non-leaders get caught up in the petty details and mundane annoyances. Indeed, you may hear some of your coworkers complain that certain tasks or projects seem not to relate to their job, or "don't matter anyway." Leaders, however, understand that everything matters, everything relates. In terms of a company's overall health, the secretary, janitor, CEO, and marketing specialist are all equally important because they each contribute to the company's vision and excellence. Excellent leaders are therefore able to see beyond small details and have appreciation for the big picture.

Principle #135

Don't doubt yourself.

While good leaders are not stubborn in their decisions, they don't waste time doubting themselves. Wishy-washy behavior is not becoming of excellent leaders and fails to inspire confidence in those around them. Champion tennis player and social activist Arthur Ashe once said, "A wise person decides slowly but abides by these decisions." Take his advice the next time you are faced with a decision. Gather all the facts, consider all the angles, take your time, and make your best decision— and most importantly, don't look back. Having confidence to make the best decision with the information available is part and parcel of developing strong leadership skills.

Principle #136

Take more of the blame
and less of the credit.

As a leader, you will be in charge of efforts that are both wildly successful and ones that tank. In the case of each, it is important to bear an appropriate amount of blame and credit. Should a project succeed, take just some of the credit. Reserve most of it for the people you successfully led. Should a project fail, however, be willing to absorb most of the blame. As psychologist Arnold H. Glasgow once put it, "A good leader takes a little more than his share of the blame, a little less than his share of the credit." Doing so will cast you as a gracious and noble leader.

Principle #137

Exude confidence.

Your self-confidence is the biggest indicator of how successful a leader you will be. How good you feel about yourself informs the degree of success you will have when undertaking projects, tasks, and responsibilities. It also determines the way you are viewed by others. Studies consistently show that people with high self-esteem are more successful, well-liked, and more effective in every aspect of their lives. Learn to believe you are a capable person. Use your self-confidence to win the trust and respect of others. Above all, know you have the stuff to lead others. As Adlai Stevenson once put it, "It's hard to lead a cavalry charge if you think you look funny on a horse."

Principle #138

Know that leadership is a skill in itself.

A commonly made mistake in many companies is promoting someone to a leadership position simply because she excelled at their previous job. While someone who excels at her job has probably mastered the skills required of that particular position, it is a mistake to assume that he will be a good leader. Indeed, leadership is a skill in itself. It involves being visionary, an excellent communicator, a swift decider, and willing to take responsibility. As H. Ross Perot once said, "Inventories can be managed, but people must be led." In other words, it takes a very particular type of person to be a leader—assess whether you have the skills or not before you take on a position of leadership.

Principle #139

Know the ins and outs
of everyone else's job.

A leader in a company is much like the director of a play—her job is to successfully guide everyone to work in concert toward a particular goal. You cannot be an effective director, however, if you don't know what is involved at every level of production. You can't help others do their job better if you are not clear on what their job is in the first place. Therefore, become familiar with jobs other than yours. Learn the flow of goods, services, and information. Understand what happens before a product gets to you, and when it leaves you. Seeing the operation in its entirety is the only way to successfully lead it.

Principle #140

Never lead with an iron fist.

Too many people in positions of power confuse leadership with dictatorship. They think that leading others means bossing them around, making unreasonable demands, or even scaring them into getting the job done. But the best leaders *inspire* others to a job well done, never frighten or bully them into it. In fact, one of America's greatest leaders, Dwight D. Eisenhower, understood this point about leadership. Both as a general and a president, he knew the difference between authoritarianism and leadership, and thus said, "You do not lead by hitting people over the head—that's assault, not leadership." Follow Eisenhower's lead by never leading with an iron fist.

Principle #141

Be willing to be lonely at the top.

---- ✳ ----

Journalist Herbert B. Swope famously quipped, "I cannot give you the formula for success, but I can give you the formula for failure, which is: Try to please everybody." Indeed, the best leaders know it is impossible to please everyone, and must therefore be willing to make difficult choices and tough calls. They must be dedicated to making right decisions, not necessarily the popular ones. Should you be forced to make an unpopular decision, mitigate the blow by communicating with the disappointed party. Explain the reasons for your decision, and offer to work with them to come to terms with it. Above all, be willing to be lonely in some of your hardest moments of leadership.

Principle #142

Be a source of inspiration.

———————— ✳ ————————

Leaders come in all different packages. Some are politicians and statesmen; others are artists and musicians. Still others are theologians, teachers, or military commanders. But no matter the context, all leaders share one common quality: the ability to inspire others to act. As John Quincy Adams, a great leader of his own time, once said, "If your actions inspire others to dream more, learn more, do more and become more, you are a leader." If you are to be a leader, you must become a source of inspiration. Look for inspiration in your family, hardships you have overcome, trips you have taken, or your relationship with God. No matter where your inspiration comes from, make sure it is genuine.

Principle #143

Understand you are only as good as the people you lead.

Everyone knows Sir Isaac Newton as the scientist who articulated the principle of gravity and the laws of motion. These and other achievements in 2005 led the Royal Society of London for the Improvement of Natural Knowledge to name him one of the most influential scientists of all times. Yet Newton knew that his accomplishments, though impressive, were the cumulative result of others that had come before him. As he put it, "If I have seen farther than others, it is because I was standing on the shoulders of giants." Indeed, the best leaders know they are only as good as the people who have contributed to their success.

MASTERING PUBLIC SPEAKING
AND PRESENTATION SKILLS

Public speaking and making presentations are skills you must master if you want to excel at your job. In fact, public speaking expert Paul B. Evans has found that 87 percent of a person's earning potential is directly linked to her ability to speak publicly and give presentations. Clearly, to be successful at work, you will need to learn to speak publicly and make presentations.

Enhancing these skills will benefit even more than your paycheck. Public speaking is about being able to communicate what you've learned about a topic. It is about being able to articulate your thoughts, feelings, and ideas, and connect them in ways that will be useful or inspirational to others. Yet most Americans avoid public speaking and making presentations. In fact, the fear of public speaking is so universal that comedian Jerry Seinfeld has joked, "Surveys show that the number one fear of Americans is public speaking. Number two is death. That means that at a funeral, the average American would rather be in the casket than doing the eulogy." Why is public speaking so widely feared? Even when people are prepared, it can be difficult to stand up in front of a table of coworkers or an audience full of people you don't know. Studies show that as many as 85 percent of the population experiences sweaty palms, a racing heart, and an upset stomach before giving a speech. Interestingly, the cause of our anxiety tends not to be the audience we face or the message we deliver—almost always, the fear of public speaking is caused by being afraid to feel afraid.

The principles in this chapter will improve your ability to speak in public and make presentations. They will help you impart your ideas in an effective and confident manner. The benefits that come from mastering this skill are immeasurable. As very few people are able to give effective presentations, you will be ahead of the pack by incorporating the following tips, tricks, and ideas into your next presentation.

Principle #144

Get over your fear of public speaking.

If you are an American, it is likely you fear public speaking. Polls, studies, and surveys consistently find that Americans fear public speaking more than spiders, bankruptcy, divorce, and even death. But public speaking needn't be the vile fate most of us think it to be. In fact, learning to be a good public speaker can improve your communication skills, make you known to people who might offer you work, and even increase your salary. Public speaking skills are useful for giving presentations, but also for conducting confident, persuasive, one-on-one conversations. So conquer your fear of public speaking—you have much to gain at work and in every other area of your life.

Principle #145

Match your outfit to your presentation.

— ❊ —

Dressing properly for a public speaking engagement is as important as the words you say. People will be less likely to take you seriously if your ensemble is distracting or does not match the tone of your presentation. If giving a business presentation, dress in solemn business attire. If giving a tour of a facility, wear clothes that allow you to move with ease. Above all, never wear attire that is loud, sexy, overly fashionable, or otherwise inappropriate. As the English composer John Newton once advised, "Dress and conduct yourself so that people who have been in your company will not recall what you had on." When speaking publicly, make sure they remember your words and not your outfit.

Principle #146

Know your audience.

———— ✳ ————

Knowing who will be listening to your presentation is the single most important thing you can do to make it a success. All the time and effort you put into your presentation will be wasted if you do not take your audience into account. Think of what your audience members need to know, and speak specifically to that need. Consider the vocabulary they have, and speak at that level. Use what you know of them to make your ideas applicable to them. Is their attendance mandatory, or voluntary? Will most of them be attending after a meal, when they are likely to be more tired? Your messages will be received more successfully than had you failed to get inside your audience's head.

Principle #147

Make your presentations in smaller rooms.

Make your presentations personal by speaking in a small space. Smaller rooms create an intimate atmosphere, which will heighten the energy of your presentation and enhance the interest of your audience. Speaking in a smaller space will also allow you to make eye contract with your audience, an important personal touch. If 25 people are expected to attend your presentation, find a space with a maximum capacity of 30 instead of 100. A small crowd will seem more impressive than an empty hall. People will be more inclined to remember a full house rather than an auditorium of empty seats.

Principle #148

Visit the site of your speaking engagement in advance.

Don't make your presentation the first time you set foot in your speaking environment. Visit the site of your presentation ahead of time. Get to know the layout, acoustics, and general feel of the space. If you know in advance that the podium is short, you can take measures to either fix the problem or alter your presentation to be podium-free so it's not a distraction to you or the audience. The size of the space will also help determine how big your gestures and how loud your voice should be. Finally, visiting the space will enable you to visualize the site of your future success in advance.

Principle #149

Pay attention to your body language.

According to *The Total Communicator*, a public speaking online magazine published by the Executive Communications Group, more than 50 percent of a person's success as a speaker is determined by his body language. In general, public speakers should stand facing their audience. They should move slowly around their presentation area rather than being planted in one spot. Gesturing is encouraged, so use your hands to flesh out your points—they should never be stuffed in your pockets or hanging limply at your sides. If you need something to focus your hands on, hold a laser pointer or other presentation device.

PRINCIPLE #150

Practice your presentation at least 5 times.

It is tempting to assume that Apple CEO, Steve Jobs, is a natural, casual person. After all, that's the impression he gives with his hip, friendly, and enthusiastic keynote speeches. But he has readily admitted that the comfort and informality he is able to achieve comes only after hours of practicing his speeches. Learn to come off as a comfortable speaker by practicing in advance. Time yourself, and practice speaking slowly. Go over pronunciation, and review all props and audiovisuals in advance. Train yourself to eliminate the "ums" and "uhs" of your speech. The more you practice, the more successful your delivery will be.

Principle #151

Integrate stories into your presentation.

Anecdotes—personalized stories that make the point of the topic you are covering—are an excellent vehicle for delivering information to others. Research has shown that people listen more intently to anecdotes than to other kinds of information (such as facts, statistics, or studies) because they can personally relate to them. Use anecdotes to talk to your audience, rather than merely lecturing to them. Tell personal stories that underscore your main points. Stories allow both you and the audience to get lost in a moment, making your presentation become a true experience. In this way they will be more likely to remember your message.

Principle #152

Be prepared to ad-lib.

Speeches benefit from improvisation—it helps a speaker come off as more natural and comfortable with her topic. Therefore, leave some wiggle room in your speech for improvisation. Take the time to elaborate on a point (although keep your time limit in mind). Use on-the-spot wit and critical thinking to acknowledge a distraction, such as a loud ceiling fan or an overactive air conditioner. Addressing these distractions naturally can provide humor relief and demystify the distraction. You can get the hang of ad-libbing by practicing your speeches in different locations to get a sense of what you might need to think quickly about if this were the real thing.

PRINCIPLE #153

Make them chuckle.

Enhance your presentation with a bit of humor. Public speaking expert Joanna Slan, author of *Using Stories and Humor to Grab Your Audience*, says, "Modern audiences expect presentations that tickle their funny bones while delivering content, and professional speakers have been forced to rise to the challenge or lose their spot on the podium." Indeed, being funny helps your audience accept you and stay interested in your presentation. It helps smooth over potentially awkward moments and makes your presentation more memorable. Avoid going overboard with the jokes, however, your job is to speak on a topic, not become a standup comedian.

Principle #154

Keep your message simple.

If you are asked to present on an issue, it is likely an important one. Important issues are often complex and multifaceted —but it is critical that your presentation not be. If your presentation is too complicated, you will lose your audience. Therefore, stick to a few main points. Use clear, simple language to ensure your message will be understood by every member of the audience. You would not want a big word to distract anyone from getting one of the most important points of your presentation. If you want to cover ideas in more depth, prepare a handout that contains more information. Or, make yourself available after the presentation to speak at length about a particular issue.

Principle #155

Bookend your presentation with a strong beginning and ending.

Capture your audience's attention with a strong opening and closing. The goal of starting and ending strong is to make good first and last impressions—it helps sell the audience on your messages. Avoid generic openers such as, "I'm here to talk to you today about..." The audience members know what you're here to talk about—otherwise they wouldn't be here to listen to you. Find new and edgy ways to grab their attention. Start them off on the edge of their seats. Likewise, deliver an ending that inspires or leaves them wanting more. These touches will make your presentation a memorable success.

Principle #156

Use props and audiovisuals.

No matter how groundbreaking your message, audiences generally need their attention recaptured every 2 to 4 minutes. Audiovisuals and props are excellent tools with which to keep people interested. Arrive early to ensure that all the equipment you need is there and in working order. Use music, sound effects, charts, graphs, and other stimuli to get your message across. Hand out samples that appeal to the sense of touch or taste to drive home a particularly important point. Anything you can do to appeal to the senses perks an audience up, resulting in a more successful presentation.

Principle #157

Involve your audience.

An involved audience is an engaged audience. During and after your presentation, it is smart to throw questions out to the audience. It helps them stay actively engaged with the presentation, and forces them to listen so they are prepared to respond if called upon. You can also physically involve them by asking for volunteers to help demonstrate a particular point. Finally, always leave time for a question and answer session at the end of your speech. It is the last chance you have to clarify your main points and engage your audience. Involving your audience can make your presentation seem more like a conversation and less like a lecture.

BALANCING WORK
AND FAMILY LIFE

No one can truly excel at his or her job without successfully balancing the needs of his or her career with the needs of his or her family. In fact, both employees and employers stand to lose when this importance balance cannot be struck.

According to Dennis J. Moberg, professor of management at Santa Clara University, people who fail to achieve a work-family balance have increased levels of stress and stress-related illness; lower life satisfaction; higher rates of family strife, domestic violence, and divorce; and increased incidence of substance abuse. Says Human Resources Development Canada, which studies work-life balance issues for that nation, "When employees are 'out of balance,' they experience more stress and fatigue and tend to be absent from work more often due to these reasons. They have less focus while at work because they are worried about issues at home and they are also more distracted at home because work matters weigh on their minds. The result is that neither situation is healthy or productive; in short, it's a lose/lose situation for employees, their families and their employer."

Companies are getting better at understanding that workers who must choose between their job and their family are less productive, more stressed, and produce lower quality work than those who don't. They tend to have higher rates of absenteeism and turnover. This means lost profits and millions spent training new people. That's why in the 21st century it has become common for companies to adopt programs that help facilitate a healthy balance between work and family.

One company that benefited from improved work-family support programs was a national bank headquartered in Tennessee. Instead of viewing the family as a side note to a person's career, bank managers began treating the family as a strategic business investment. They trained their employees to integrate their families into their work lives. They allowed them to be flexible with their schedules and take advantage of child care vouchers and work events that were geared around the whole family. Astonishingly, managers found that the sectors of the bank that were most supportive of work-family balance initiatives retained employees twice as long as the bank's average, and kept 7 percent more of their repeat customers. These gains contributed to a 55 percent profit gain, or an additional $106 million in profits over 2 years!

Indeed, work-family balance programs have been proven to offer a wide range of benefits for both employer and employee. Among these are the ability to attract and retain the best employees; improve morale among workers; lower rates of sickness, absenteeism, and turnover; reduce new employee training costs; improve company loyalty; enhance relationships between colleagues; build better teamwork skills; increase levels of productivity; and decrease levels of stress and burn-out. All of these translate into higher company profits and higher job satisfaction for employees.

Excelling at your job means balancing your professional responsibilities with your family's needs, goals, and desires. The following simple principles will help you make sure you are giving enough to both your job and your family.

Principle #158

"Re-hire" yourself.

Too many people find themselves working 60-hour weeks with no bonus or extra pay. Their days, nights, and weekends are spent catching up on e-mail and making callbacks. If this sounds like your life, ask yourself: was this the job you signed on for? Has it morphed beyond the responsibilities you were initially prepared to take on? If the answer is "yes," it is time to "re-hire" yourself. Re-hiring oneself, according to University of Southern California business professor Warren Bennis, is the important process of clarifying the scope and expectations of your job with your manager, and renegotiating if necessary. Rewriting your job description is helpful for those who need to ensure they are compensated fairly for the time they put in, as well as those seeking to tame their out-of-control job.

PRINCIPLE #159

Share your calendar with your family.

A classic example of the workaholic parent is the mom or dad who forgets that the annual sales meeting is the same day as Susie's piano recital or Billy's soccer game. Missing your loved ones' events and milestones can threaten even the closest families. Avoid scheduling conflicts by sharing your work calendar with your family. Keep it posted in the kitchen or living room and update it regularly. By clearly labeling after-hours appointments, weekend meetings, or business trips, you can avoid forcing your family to play second fiddle to your job. Also, look into sharing calendars electronically— many e-mail programs, such as Outlook and Google mail, allow you to merge e-calendars with others.

Principle #160

Investigate how your company can help you balance work and family.

Companies are more responsive than ever to their employees' desire to balance their responsibilities at work and home. Studies show that when companies offer work-family support, they see lower turnover and absenteeism rates, and higher productivity and satisfaction. Since all these factors translate into higher profits, companies are interested in supporting your goal of balancing work and family. Find out if your company offers any of the following work-family support programs: childcare, flex hours, job-sharing, eldercare initiatives, telecommuting, compressed work weeks (such as working four 10-hour days instead of five 8-hour days), and time-management seminars.

PRINCIPLE #161

Avoid bringing work home on weekends.

Most jobs require that people take work home at least occasionally. But if your take-home work is interfering with your domestic relationships and responsibilities, it's time to draw the line. Put limits on the nature and quantity of work you allow yourself to bring home by carving out time to spend just with family. Avoid bringing work home on weekends, especially if you have children. Try and limit weekday evening meetings and events to 1 or 2 per week, and weekend events or business trips to 1 or 2 per month. Check e-mail from home only after the kids are asleep, or during time when everyone is doing solitary activities.

Principle #162

Take all paid vacation you are offered.

Vacation time is difficult to come by in America—the average worker gets just 14 days off per year. This is paltry compared to European nations such as Britain (where the average is 24 days) or France (where the average is 39 days). More astonishing, however, is the number of American workers who choose not to take advantage of the paid vacation they are offered. According to a 2006 study by Expedia.com, American workers collectively give back 175 million paid vacation days to their employers every year. If you are offered paid vacation, give yourself and your family a much needed break by using it. Even if you don't have the funds or desire to travel, spend time at home together as a family.

PRINCIPLE #163

Control your personal digital assistant rather than letting it control you.

Each year, Americans make increasing use of personal digital assistants (PDAs) such as cell phones and BlackBerries. On the one hand, these devices can offer more balance between work and family by allowing you to respond to e-mails and messages away from the office. Yet more often, PDAs muddle a healthy separation between work and family life, functioning as a leash that keeps you working far beyond the typical 8-hour work day. You'll have to decide for yourself whether your devices are freeing or imprisoning you. Make sure to turn your PDA off during important family time such as dinner and vacation.

Principle #164

Integrate your family
into your work life.

An old saying goes, "If the mountain will not come to Muhammad, then Muhammad will go to the mountain." In other words, sometimes the best way to make a situation work is to accommodate it, rather than waiting for it to resolve on its own. If your job interferes with time spent with your family, incorporate your family into your job. Always bring family members to company events such as picnics or holiday parties. Involve them in conferences or workshops, either as helpers or observers. Experiencing business-related events together is a great way to integrate your family into your work life when your work life cannot be interrupted.

PRINCIPLE #165

Bring a good mood home with you.

A bad mood is like an infectious disease—it travels with you, and can contaminate others. When you leave work in a bad mood, time reserved for your family becomes infected by that mood. Mary K. Lawler and Jo Robertson, professors of human development at of Oklahoma State University, have researched the transferable affect of both good and bad moods. "Positive and negative feelings go with you to work and to home," they explain. "When things are going well at home, you go to work knowing your family life is under control. On the other hand, you may come home after a difficult day at work ready for an argument at home." Keep family time enjoyable by bringing home good moods from work.

PRINCIPLE #166

Keep in touch, even when you can't be there.

There will be times you won't be able to help missing family functions and events due to work. Let your family know you care during these times by keeping touch. During breaks, call home. Use speakerphone to facilitate the feeling of being there. If you're away on business, send postcards and upload pictures so your family feels like they are there with you. Have your children fax or e-mail homework they need help with. Have big events you missed videotaped, and post them on YouTube, or watch them together when you're back. Keeping in touch when you can't be there will mean a lot to your family, and cut down on the amount to catch up on when you get home.

PRINCIPLE #167

Make your working hours count.

———————————— ❋ ————————————

Someone who works 50 to 60 hours a week does not necessarily produce better quality, or even more work, than someone who puts in 40 hours a week. In fact, a 2006 report produced by Australian researchers found that employees who put in 10- to 12-hour days experienced decreased alertness, memory and attention compared to workers who put in 8-hour days. The researchers argued that offices that encourage long hours and overtime tend to have lower levels of productivity per employee hour worked. Indeed, it doesn't make sense to work overtime just to feed the illusion that you are doing more than others. Instead, work efficiently by producing higher quality work in less time. Your boss—and your family—will appreciate it.

Principle #168

Be home in time for family dinner.

Your family's dinner conversations may not be earth-shattering, but simply the act of sitting down together for 30 minutes each day goes a long way toward enhancing your family's mental, physical, and academic health. In fact, a 2006 report released by Columbia University found that families who eat together experience lower levels of drug abuse, smoking, and partying, and higher levels of academic achievement, than families who do not. Therefore, make it a priority to be home in time for family dinner every single night. If you have to, get into work earlier than normal so you leave earlier to ensure you are home in time for dinner.

Principle #169

Hold family meetings.

An excellent way to stay on the same page with your busy family is to hold weekly or monthly family meetings. Use these meetings to set family priorities, values, and standards. Topics for discussion can include how many work hours are too many; who should be responsible for household tasks; and ideas how the family might spend more time together. It is important to set aside specific meeting times to discuss these issues, rather than randomly broaching them over dinner or other events. Carving out special time to dedicate to conversations about the functioning of the family will ensure they get discussed, and help all family members feel like they have a voice in the conversation.

Principle #170

Avoid taking work with you on vacation.

— ❋ —

Give yourself and your family a much needed break by using your vacation time only for vacation. Not only do American workers get less vacation time than their counterparts in other nations, but studies show that increasing numbers take work with them when they do manage to get away. According to a 2007 study by CareerBuilder.com, 20 percent of Americans take work with them while on vacation. Interestingly, however, only 9 percent of workers say their employers expect them to work on vacation. Bringing your office with you on vacation interrupts quality time you should be spending with your family and prevents you from resting and recharging. The next time you take a vacation, make it a true break from work.

PRINCIPLE #171

Assess whether the job is truly right for you.

If you are unable to achieve a work-family balance, it may be time to assess whether you are in the right position. No job is worth jeopardizing your relationship with your family, and no employer worth working for would ask you to do so. As children's rights activist Marian Wright Edelman has advised, "Never work just for money or for power. They won't save your soul or help you sleep at night." If you find yourself needing to choose between your career and your family, discuss with your spouse how to move forward. Options could include taking a different position within your company, stepping down from management, or seeking a new job altogether.

Pursuing Education and Professional Advancement

Educating yourself is guaranteed to pay off professionally. According to a 2004 report by the U.S. Department of Commerce, those with no high school education earn an average of $26,879 per year. Those with a high school diploma earn a bit more, about $37,031 per year. Spending four years in college and earning a bachelor's degree, however, puts a person's average annual salary at $67,495. Put another way, a 2007 College Board Study found that people with a bachelor's degree earn over 60 percent more than those with only a high school diploma. Over a lifetime, the gap in earning potential between a high school diploma and a bachelor's is more than $800,000!

There is even more money to be made if you advance academically beyond the college level. According to the National At-Risk Education Network, a master's degree is worth an additional $13,000 per year. Furthermore, bachelor's and master's degree holders are more likely to be consistently employed, work in better conditions, receive better benefits, travel more, and have more professional interests than those who cap their education earlier.

But a formal academic experience is not the only way to educate yourself in ways that will help you excel at your job. In fact, there is a whole world of professional development opportunities that can enhance your career. Professional development takes many forms. It can be classes, lectures, or training events sponsored by your company. It can be workshops at conferences. Furthermore, the Internet has made it possible to take online classes and seminars that can dramatically increase your skill set in a matter of hours.

Educating yourself on a variety of fronts will vastly benefit your career. The following principles underscore the importance of making education an ongoing part of your professional life, and will help you excel at and advance through your career.

Principle #172

Attend conferences.

❊

Conferences are an excellent way to further your professional education and development. The typical conference features industry leaders speaking and presenting about innovations in the field; skill-building workshops and seminars; and hands-on demonstrations of new products and services. As the English lawyer and philosopher Francis Bacon once said, "Reading maketh a full man; conference a ready man; and writing an exact man." When you do go to a conference, be sure to bring lots of business cards, as it is an excellent place to network and make new connections.

Principle #173

Learn about other cultures.

In our increasingly diverse world, those unfamiliar with other cultures are viewed as ignorant, and are rarely able to excel at their job. It is likely that to do your job, you need to interface with people from different religions, ethnicities, and nationalities, either through your contacts with coworkers, distributors, vendors, suppliers, or clients. Being comfortable with people different from you is an important skill to build. If you have the resources, traveling is an excellent way to learn about other cultures. Or, read books or search the Internet on different countries or religions. Eat in ethnic restaurants. By educating yourself about different customs, you gain a better understanding of audiences you might encounter professionally.

Principle #174

Read trade magazines.

In the U.S. alone, thousands of magazines exist that serve particular industries. Called "trade" magazines, their content is intended for professionals within a certain industry. Trade magazines exist for fields as varied as education, healthcare, publishing, information technology, construction, retail, sales and marketing, development, food and beverage, insurance, multimedia, energy, and many more. They feature industry-related articles about new advancements, ways to make your business more effective, and what the competition is up to. By keeping abreast of the latest developments, you are likely to become a more competitive expert in your field.

Principle #175

Learn another language.

As the demographics of industry change, so does the language in which business is conducted. Now more than ever, companies need employees who can communicate in other languages. Experts predict that due to changing market demographics and the rising importance of China, India, and Middle Eastern nations to a variety of industries, there will be a great demand for Arabic, Mandarin, and Hindi speakers. Learning one of these languages will put you well ahead of the pack in just about any job you seek that has international interests. Within the United States, companies continue to seek employees who are fluent or proficient in Spanish. Learning another language can do wonders for your career both at home and abroad.

Principle #176

Get a higher degree.

A surefire way to excel at your job and make more money is to get a higher degree. That's because education pays—literally. In 2004, the average full-time employee with a high school diploma earned less than $30,000 annually. Those with a bachelor's degree, however, earned upwards of $60,000, and those with a master's degree pulled in more than $73,000 per year. Although the cost of college and professional degree programs increase every year, the investment in your future is worth it. As humorist Andy McIntyre once quipped, "If you think education is expensive, try ignorance."

PRINCIPLE #177

Investigate whether your company will pay you to go to school.

It seems too good to be true—your company continuing to pay your salary, and your tuition, while you go to school? Yet many companies are more than willing to invest in the education of their employees, because it means they'll have smarter, more capable people working for them. Most often, employees who get an employer-sponsored degree must sign a contract saying they'll continue to work for the company for 1, 2, even 5 years after they earn their degree, or else pay back the tuition they spent. But assuming you are willing to indenture yourself, charging your degree to your employer can work out well for both of you.

Principle #178

Build your skill set.

The new word to describe American labor is "skilled." As non-skilled jobs close down or are moved abroad, jobs that remain in the United States require a more highly skilled work force than ever. According to the Department of Labor, in 2000, 65 percent of jobs required new skills. By 2005, that figure had jumped to 85 percent. Clearly, expanding your skill set is import if you want to excel at your job. Some of the most highly sought-after skills include computer and information technology, nursing, mastery of a foreign language, and management. Work on building your abilities in these and other areas.

Principle #179

Take a one-time seminar.

Education doesn't have to take years and cost thousands. In fact, all around the United States, one-time seminars are springing up that teach people a new skill in just a few hours and for minimal cost. The Learning Annex is one company that offers seminars in multiple American cities. For about the price of a good meal, students can take seminars in accounting, publishing, business management, law, public speaking, and other areas. For an extra fee, one can often get a certificate showing completion of the seminar, which can look great on your office wall or in your "promote-me" file. Consider one-time seminars when you are looking to build your skill set for a new job or the one you already have.

Principle #180

Seek out professional development programs.

———————— ❊ ————————

Learning and enrichment doesn't have to come in the form of a formal degree from an academic institution. In fact, most job-related training and knowledge comes from the professional realm rather than lessons learned in a classroom. Professional development programs may be offered by your employer or at industry-related events. Take advantage of such opportunities whenever you can. You will expose yourself to "industry street smarts" that will give you the leg up in your field. Taking the initiative to develop your skills through professional development programs will put your career on a fast track to success.

Principle #181

Shadow someone with more experience than you.

For some jobs, there are no classes. To learn what there is to know, shadow someone with more experience than you. As you experience challenges, failures, and successes, this person will be there to give advice, pick you up, and celebrate. When choosing someone to shadow, select someone you respect. It is ideal that this person share your interests and goals. If you have trouble selecting someone, turn to professional connections you already have. Research your alumni directory. See if local organizations can offer you a person in the industry to shadow, or ask your human resources department to pair you up with someone.

Principle #182

Mentor someone else.

Sharing your wisdom and knowledge with someone just starting out is an excellent way to reinforce what you already know. Furthermore, acting as a mentor helps to continually develop skills in your area of expertise. Sometimes we get so bogged down in our fields that we lose sight of the bigger picture and purpose. Acting as a mentor, however, can bring fresh perspective by challenging you to articulate ideas you have yet to express. Even if you feel jaded in your field, the enthusiasm you will feel from the person you mentor will be a positive reminder of why you chose your industry in the first place.

Principle #183

Improve your vocabulary.

In professional settings, people judge others by the words they use to express themselves. If you use simple words or mispronounce words, coworkers will view you as a simple and uneducated person. On the other hand, if you use overly complex words, people will sense you are trying to sound more intelligent than you are. Therefore, in order to excel at your job and be respected by your coworkers, you must build a solid vocabulary. Sign up with an online resource that will e-mail you a word a day, or buy a word-of-the-day calendar. Write down words you don't know and look them up. As Winston Churchill once stated, "A good vocabulary will be of service throughout your life."

Principle #184

Make the commute your classroom.

— ✳ —

The average American commutes almost an hour a day to get to work. Many of us waste that hour being frustrated with traffic or trying to avoid staring at people packed on our train. Instead of losing an hour of your day, make the commute your classroom. Use your car stereo, walkman, or iPod to listen to audiobooks, podcasts, or news stories of business-related events. Get voice-activated technology that allows you to record tasks you don't want to forget about, or ideas that come to you on the spot. In time your commute will no longer be the stressful event you once dreaded, but something you wish lasted a couple minutes longer.

Principle #185

Take a software class.

All forms of business are increasingly conducted using office suite software such as Microsoft Word and Excel, or Adobe Photoshop or InDesign. Your career will be stunted if you are unable to use these programs with precision and ease. Investigate whether your local community college offers adult education courses in these and other software programs. Just a few sessions will have you feeling confident in your technological abilities. Being fluent in computer programs is especially important for independent contractors who must be willing and able to work in whatever program the client wants.

CHANGING CAREERS

Sometimes, the best thing you can do for your career is to change it. Switching careers is a more modern, but acceptable, response to a static or unsatisfying job. In decades past, Americans were more likely to get one job and stick with it. But times have changed: according to the Bureau of Labor Statistics, average Americans now changes jobs 10 times in the course of their lifetime. Furthermore, they average about 3 career switches over the course of their working life.

For as many Americans who make the big change, even more dream about doing it. According to a nationwide online survey of more than 6,000 working adults by University of Phoenix, nearly one quarter of working adults—23 percent—are considering a career switch at any given moment. Their number one reason? They feel that their current careers fail to enrich them on a daily basis. Indeed, 61 percent said they thought a career change would offer "the opportunity to do something more fulfilling."

But not everyone has the courage to make a career change. According to 66 percent of respondents in the University of Phoenix survey, financial issues have kept them from switching careers. They worry they will not earn as much if they have to start at the bottom of a new field. Others fear they may be unemployed in between their current position and a new one. The second reason people gave for why they don't make a career change was because they are too busy and confused by the process. Indeed, about a third of respondents (36 percent) cite "not enough time" and "not knowing where to start" as why they would not switch careers. Finally, 30 percent said family issues and commitments have prevented them from changing careers.

While it is not to be undertaken without planning and foresight, there are times when the best thing for your career is change. Use the following principles to help you evaluate whether you need a career change, how large a change it should be, and how you should go about managing it.

Principle #186

Network your way to a new career.

According to a major career counseling company, 70 percent of all available jobs go unadvertised. This means when you look for a job, you are only viewing 30 percent of available positions! The remainder of positions are never posted, because they are filled through word of mouth—otherwise known as networking. If you want to change careers, network with people in different industries. Ask what they like and hate about their job. Ask about the conditions in which they work (salary, vacation, responsibilities, stress levels, etc.). Let people in these industries know you are considering a career change, and to contact you should they hear of any opportunities.

Principle #187

Write a personal mission statement.

※

Changing careers will require you to have a targeted idea of who you are and what you intend to do with your life professionally. To figure that out, write a personal mission statement. Your mission statement should be 1 or 2 sentences long. It should clearly state the things about a job that are most important to you, things that motivate you to do your best. Then, it should reflect goals based on these values. Your mission statement should be motivational, easy to understand, and action-oriented. An example might be, "Because I am passionate about animals, can stomach the sight of blood, and work well under pressure, I want to devote my life to service in the veterinary industry."

Principle #188

Make a list of your short-term career goals.

— ※ —

Changing careers may take a long time. Get the ball rolling by keeping a list of short-term goals that are related to your career change. These are goals that should be able to be accomplished on a daily or weekly basis. For example, you should have "scanning the want ads" and "taking a course to gain a new skill" on your list. Others can be tasks such as updating your résumé, joining your college's alumni networking group, or embarking on a personal journey to find your true calling. Cross items off your list as you do them to give yourself an immediate sense of accomplishment.

Principle #189

Make a list of your long-term career goals.

The decision to change careers is big, and one that has long-term implications, even potential consequences, for you and your family. To make such a big decision, you'll need to consider what your long-term goals are. Do you want to get an advanced degree? Own a business? Have time for a family? Get rich? Own a home? Travel often? Write down your long-term goals, and craft your career change around them. Your career change and all steps toward it should actively support these goals. If at any point your career change contradicts one of them, it may be the wrong move.

Principle #190

Step outside your professional safety zone.

Go outside your safety zone to expose yourself to new endeavors, industries, and opportunities. For example, if you are a desk person, try doing work out in the field; if you have always feared computers, take an IT skills class. Pushing the boundaries of your skills can open professional doors you never knew existed. During any one of these new endeavors, you will likely meet people who will unexpectedly influence you, and learn about jobs you never even knew existed. Your goal should be to have a groundbreaking experience that leads you to consider a new professional opportunity.

PRINCIPLE #191

Assess whether you need a change of pace or a complete overhaul.

Everyone experiences bouts of the job blahs now and then. Because changing careers is such a huge decision, it is important to differentiate normal boredom and restlessness with a desire to overhaul your career. To find out, ask yourself: how did I arrive at this job? Did I want it, or was it accidental? What parts of my job would I miss? Am I willing to train myself for a new career? Would a department or company switch satisfy my need for change, or am I looking for complete professional reinvention? Your answers should be able to tell you whether you need a change of pace or a complete overhaul.

Principle #192

Let yourself daydream about a new professional you.

As adults we tend to let our hopes and dreams fall by the wayside, regarding them as childish or unrealistic. But hopes and dreams are the pillars on which we can base attainable goals. Let your mind wander and see where it leads you. Perhaps you envision yourself in your company, but in a higher position or different department. Perhaps you see yourself as a restaurant owner or shopkeeper. Maybe you see yourself making a living helping others in the non-profit sector. Engage in these professional daydreams at least 3 times a week. If you keep seeing the same image after a few weeks, it could be time to make that daydream a reality.

Principle #193

Be willing to go back to school.

The most drastic career changes typically require a person to finish college, or get a first or second master's degree or more. Those contemplating big career changes are aware of this, and are usually willing to go back to school if it means reorienting themselves professionally. A survey by the University of Phoenix found that 71 percent of adults considering a career change believe that education will play a role in their career paths. Furthermore, 84 percent agree that education is important in achieving their professional goals. Getting another degree may take as little as 6 months and as long as 10 years, so research what you are getting into before signing up for classes.

PRINCIPLE #194

Consult with a career counselor.

Career counselors can be a useful resource for a person considering a career change. Career counselors are professionals who hold an advanced degree in counseling, but specialize in issues relating to careers and the job market. They excel at helping individuals articulate their strengths, weaknesses, and goals. They can also help people brainstorm about new directions they'd like to see their life take. A list of certified career counselors is available through the National Career Development Association, online at www.ncda.org or by calling 866.367.6232. If you have been considering a career change for more than 1 year, it might be time to consult a professional who can help you take the plunge.

Principle #195

Assess how much you are willing to change.

The whole point of switching careers is because you feel ready for a change. But sometimes, the idea of making a change is more appealing than actually doing all the work to accomplish the change. Before you change careers, assess the degree to which you are willing to change your life. Are you willing to relocate for a new career? Go back to school? Take a pay cut? Be out of work for a while? Work longer hours? Start from the bottom? Your answers to these questions will indicate the degree of change you are willing to accept.

Principle #196

Be realistic about your ability to change careers.

The best career changes act in concert with all other aspects of a person's life. Examine your personal life to see how realistic it is for you to make a career change. If you've just had a child, for example, or recently purchased an expensive home, it may not be the best time to go out on a limb professionally. If you are a few years from retirement, it usually makes sense to stick with the career and company you've been with. Finally, if you would need to go back to school for 7 or more years in order to make a career change, you might think twice about overhauling your professional life.

Principle #197

Make a career change that enriches your life.

According to a nationwide survey of more than 6,000 working adults by the University of Phoenix, personal fulfillment is the number one reason people make a career change. While some people changed careers to do something different or to earn more pay, 61 percent of those polled cited "the opportunity to do something more fulfilling" as the reason why they were considering a career change. Respondents were most interested in taking up do-gooder jobs in the fields of education, healthcare and medicine, and non-profit industries. If you have always wanted to do something you loved that would also make the world a better place, you are not alone: go for it!

PRINCIPLE #198

Volunteer or intern to get the feel of a new industry.

An old expression advises those considering a big change to "try the milk before you buy the cow." While this advice rings true for dating and buying a new car, it also is applicable to career changes. Spend at least 40 hours working in the industry you are considering switching to. Apply for an internship or work-study program, or volunteer to help out. Either way, you will get an inside look at what life in that industry is really like. Volunteering in an animal hospital, for example, is a great way to know whether you want to be a vet before you pay thousands and spend 4 or more years in veterinary school.

PRINCIPLE #199

Identify your transferable skills.

Transferable skills are abilities you have that enable you to move effortlessly from industry to industry. They are skills you use in one industry which will transfer over well to a new industry. The more transferable skills a person has, the easier it will be for them to make a drastic career change. Some skills that are widely transferable are: the ability to manage projects, people, and budgets; leading or participating in teams; excelling at written or verbal communication; sales expertise; training, coaching, or educating; and computer programming. List all of your transferable skills, and start imagining what other industries they might work well in.

Principle #200

Go out on a limb.

You probably know Crocs, the brightly colored, plastic, and popular clog seemingly everywhere. Indeed, Crocs have become a nationwide sensation, doing millions of dollars of business a year. But Crocs got a modest and unlikely start. The company opened after friends George Boedecker Jr., Scott Seamans, and Lyndon Hanson went on a sailing trip in the Caribbean. Inspired by their scenery, they came up with the idea to make a boating shoe that would be practical, comfortable, and funky. They never would have guessed that within a few years, Crocs would be available in major retail stores, and even internationally. Get inspired by their story, and go out on a limb with your own quirky, great idea. It might just pay off.

ADDITIONAL INFORMATION AND IDEAS

The following pages contain a few exercises that will help you excel at your job. Practicing these exercises you help you adopt a professionalism that will impress your coworkers and your managers!

These exercises will help you overcome habits that are preventing you from doing your best at work. Make a habit of performing them whenever you are feeling particularly unaccomplished. They will also help you get back on track with your short- and long-term professional goals.

Practice these exercises to become more organized, to set professional goals, to assess your skill set, to discover which skills are transferable to another position or industry, and to develop habits that will get you promoted. Each of these skills must be mastered if you are to excel at your job.

The following should be practiced daily to excel at your job:

Setting Professional Goals
This exercise will help you set both short- and long-term professional goals for this month and the next 10 years.

Tips for Getting and Staying Organized
Doing each of these tasks every single day will greatly enhance your ability to get and stay organized.

Ten Daily Habits That Can Help You Get Promoted
Implement each of these habits in your daily routine, and you are sure to be promoted in no time.

Identify Your Transferable Skills
This exercise will help you identify skills you currently possess that are required in an industry you'd like to break into.

Setting Professional Goals

Make a list of your professional goals. These will range depending on what you want to get out of your career. Do you want to work outside of an office? Do you want to be an executive? Do you want your job to involve travel, public speaking, or working in the field? Do you want teaching others to be an aspect of your professional life? Do you want to work with your hands? Include both long- and short-term goals, and break large goals into smaller, attainable goals. Use the ideas below to help you along. Write in this book so that you'll always have access to your dreams and goals, and use pencil so you can revise them as necessary.

Things I want to accomplish at my job or in my career this month.

1. _____

2. _____

3. _____

4. _____

5. _____

Things I want to accomplish at my job or in my career this quarter.

1. _____

2. _____

3. _____

4. _____

5. _____

Things I want to accomplish at my job or in my career this year.

1. _____

2. _____

3. _____

4. _____

5. _____

Things I want to accomplish at my job or in my career in the next 5 years.

1. _____

2. _____

3. _____

4. _____

5. _____

Things I want to accomplish at my job or in my career in the next 10 years.

1. _____

2. _____

3. _____

4. _____

5. _____

Tips for Getting and Staying Organized

Doing each of the following tasks every single day will greatly enhance your ability to get and stay organized.

- Start every day with a list of things that needs to get done. As you complete a task, cross it off your list.
- Check postal mail. If you can pay a bill or answer a query in under 5 minutes, do it. If not, put it in a To Do box that you will empty by Friday at 5 p.m. If this To Do box is not emptied, don't let yourself go home for the weekend.
- Check voice mails. Leave all calls you can't return marked as unheard.
- Check e-mail. Leave all messages you can't return marked as unread.
- Split your day up, making certain hours devoted solely to certain tasks. For example, make 8 to 9 a.m. the time during which you review and answer messages, e-mails and mail. Make 9 to 11 a.m. the time during which you work uninterrupted on a project. Make 11 a.m. to noon the time during which you hold office hours; this

is the time when colleagues should know to reach you. Carve out your day as needed.

- Keep your day planner with you at all times. Write down all appointments. Block out travel time. Carve out time you need to do specific work. When you write down an appointment, also write down a contact phone number and address so you have all the information you need together.

- End each day by looking at your list of things that needed to get done. If there are any tasks you did not get to, circle them. These will go at the top of your list for tomorrow.

Ten Daily Habits That Can Get You Promoted

If you implement just one of the following habits in your workday, you are bound to be promoted in no time. Remember, managers are more likely to promote workers that have proven themselves indispensable to the operation. This involves being dependable, creative, hard-working, innovative, and taking initiative.

1) Ask your manager for more responsibility or a new project.
2) Show up to work 20 minutes early and stay 20 minutes late.
3) Let your boss know you are interested in being promoted.
4) Ask your human resources representative if there are any higher-level openings in your department or in another department in your company.
5) Solve a problem for your boss.
6) Write down all the things you accomplished at work this week, including anything notable, such as if they were done especially quickly or saved the company money.
7) Find someone at your company to mentor you.
8) Research the market value of your position at other companies around the country.
9) Sign up for a seminar, conference, or class that will give you a new skill.
10) Ask someone at your workplace who was recently promoted how she did it.

Identify Your Transferable Skills

In this exercise, you will identify your transferable skills. These are skills, tools, or talents you have developed in one industry that could transfer over well to a new one. People with many transferable skills have an easier time making a career change because they are already equipped with talents and knowledge that will help them succeed in a new industry (and be hired in one, despite having little direct experience in the field). Some skills that are widely transferable are: the ability to lead a team, manage projects, oversee people, and stick to budgets. Other transferable skills include having exceptional written or verbal communication skills; sales expertise; experience training, coaching, or educating; and being able to work with computers. To identify your transferable skills, list them in the box below. Match them up to skills that are needed in an industry you'd like to move to. This will help you assess whether you have the skills required to switch industries.

Skills Required for My Target Industry	Skills I Currently Have
_____	_____
_____	_____
_____	_____
_____	_____
_____	_____

If you don't have many skills that are exactly transferable, think about which skills you possess that would be adaptable to a new industry. For example, if you have worked your whole life at a software design office, you may not have many skills that transfer over to the field of medicine. But if your job was particularly high stress, or you worked on medical software, these skills might be adaptable to a career in medicine.

CONCLUSION

Congratulations! By now, you should feel good about your prospects for excelling at your job, and even for getting promoted. *Simple Principles™ to Excel at Your Job* has helped you develop good work habits, communicate effectively, gain the respect of your colleagues, position yourself for promotion and advancement, negotiate a better package for yourself at work, avoid burnout, sidestep classic on-the-job mistakes, and recognize your need to change careers. If you have followed the hints, tips, tricks, ideas, suggestions, and other principles contained in this book, you are likely closer than ever to achieving your goal of excelling at your job. Once you have gone through this book from beginning to end, you should have a solid idea of how to apply excellent work habits to your own life. The 200 principles included in this book have shown you that every worker is capable of excelling at his or her job provided he or she is willing to show a little initiative, creativity, and work hard.

Simple Principles™ to Excel at Your Job is written to help remind you that you are capable of getting ahead in your company and in your industry. You are capable of switching fields if you want. You are capable of loving the process of going to work, working as a team, and becoming a leader in your company or organization. Even if you find certain skills daunting or difficult, you can get better at them by applying the principles contained in this book.

Practice what you have learned. Keep this book handy and refer to it when you need a reminder. The key thing to remember is that an outstanding, interesting, and successful career is completely within your grasp if you just open yourself up to this new way of thinking. Remember, you can excel in your job! We wish you all the best in your professional endeavors.

TELL US YOUR STORY

Simple Principles™ to Excel at Your Job has changed the lives of countless people, helping them make more money, have more power, and advance in their careers faster than they ever imagined. Now we want to hear your story about how this book has improved your job performance.

Tell us ...
- Why did you purchase this book?
- Which areas of your job did you want to improve?
- How did this book help you improve in those areas?
- How did this book change your life?
- Which principles did you like the most?
- What did you like most about this book?
- Would you recommend this book to others?

Email us your response at info@wspublishinggroup.com or write to us at:

WS Publishing Group
7290 Navajo Road, Suite 207
San Diego, CA 92119

Please include your name and an email address and/or phone number where you can be reached.

Please let us know if WS Publishing may or may not use your story and/or name in future book titles, and if you would be interested in participating in radio or TV interviews.

Great Titles in the
SIMPLE PRINCIPLES™ SERIES

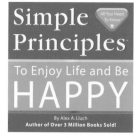

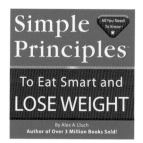

LOG ON TO **WSPUBLISHINGGROUP.COM** TO CHECK FOR
RELEASE DATES ON THESE AND FUTURE TITLES.

More Great Titles in the
SIMPLE PRINCIPLES™ SERIES

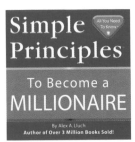

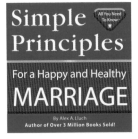

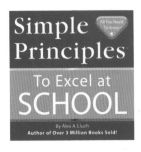

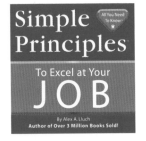

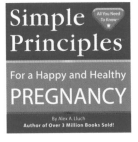

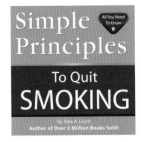

LOG ON TO/**WSPUBLISHINGGROUP**.COM TO CHECK FOR
RELEASE DATES ON THESE AND FUTURE TITLES.

Other Best-Selling Books by Alex A. Lluch

HOME & FINANCE
- The Very Best Home Improvement Guide & Document Organizer
- The Very Best Home Buying Guide & Document Organizer
- The Very Best Home Selling Guide & Document Organizer
- The Very Best Budget & Finance Guide with Document Organizer
- The Ultimate Home Journal & Organizer
- The Ultimate Home Buying Guide & Organizer

BABY JOURNALS & PARENTING
- The Complete Baby Journal Organizer & Keepsake
- Keepsake of Love Baby Journal
- Snuggle Bears Baby Journal Keepsake & Organizer
- Humble Bumbles Baby Journal
- Simple Principles to Raise a Successful Child

CHILDREN'S BOOKS
- I Like to Learn: Alphabet, Numbers, Colors & Opposites
- Alexander, It's Time for Bed!
- Do I Look Good in Color?
- Zoo Clues Animal Alphabet
- Animal Alphabet: Slide & Seek the ABC's
- Counting Chameleon
- Big Bugs, Small Bugs

LOG ON TO **WSPublishingGroup.com** TO CHECK FOR RELEASE DATES ON THESE AND FUTURE TITLES.

More Best-Selling Books
by Alex A. Lluch

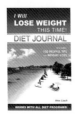

COOKING, FITNESS & DIET

- The Very Best Cooking Guide & Recipe Organizer
- Easy Cooking Guide & Recipe Organizer
- Get Fit Now! Workout Journal
- Lose Weight Now! Diet Journal & Organizer
- I Will Lose Weight This Time! Diet Journal
- The Ultimate Pocket Diet Journal

WEDDING PLANNING

- The Ultimate Wedding Planning Kit
- The Complete Wedding Planner & Organizer
- Easy Wedding Planner, Organizer & Keepsake
- Easy Wedding Planning Plus
- Easy Wedding Planning
- The Ultimate Wedding Workbook & Organizer
- The Ultimate Wedding Planner & Organizer
- Making Your Wedding Beautiful, Memorable & Unique
- Planning the Most Memorable Wedding on Any Budget
- My Wedding Journal, Organizer & Keepsake
- The Ultimate Wedding Planning Guide
- The Ultimate Guide to Wedding Music
- Wedding Party Responsibility Cards

LOG ON TO **WSPUBLISHINGGROUP.COM** TO CHECK FOR
RELEASE DATES ON THESE AND FUTURE TITLES.

About the Author and Creator of the
SIMPLE PRINCIPLES™ SERIES

Alex A. Lluch is a seasoned entrepreneur with outstanding life achievements. He grew up very poor and lost his father at age 15. But through hard work and dedication, he has become one of the most successful authors and businessmen of our time. He is now using his life experience to write the Simple Principles™ series to help people improve their lives.

The following are a few of Alex's achievements:

- Author of over 3 million books sold in a wide range of categories: health, fitness, diet, home, finance, weddings, children, and babies
- President of WS Publishing Group, a successful publishing company
- President of WeddingSolutions.com, one of the world's most popular wedding planning websites
- President of UltimateGiftRegistry.com, an extensive website that allows users to register for gifts for all occasions
- President of a highly successful toy and candy company
- Has worked extensively in China, Hong Kong, Spain, Israel and Mexico
- Designed complex communication systems for Fortune 500 companies
- Black belt in Karate and Judo, winning many national tournaments
- Owns real estate in California, Colorado, Georgia and Montana
- B.S. in Electronics Engineering and an M.S. in Computer Science

Alex Lluch lives in San Diego, California with his wife of 16 years and their three wonderful children.